THE BOOKS OF THE BIBLE

The Subject, Structure, Situation, and Significant Verses of Each Book

G. Michael Cocoris

THE BOOKS OF THE BIBLE

The Subject, Structure, Situation, and Significant Verses of Each Book

G. Michael Cocoris

© 2023 by G. Michael Cocoris

All rights reserved. This publication may not be reproduced *for sale* (in whole or in part, edited, or revised) in any way, form, or means including, but not limited to, electronic, mechanical, photocopying, recording, or any kind of storage and retrieval system, except for brief quotations in printed reviews, without the written permission of G. Michael Cocoris, 2016 Euclid #20, Santa Monica, CA 90405, michaelcocoris@gmail.com, or his appointed representatives. Permission is hereby granted, however, for the reproduction of the whole or parts of the whole without changing the content in any way for *free distribution,* provided all copies contain this copyright notice in its entirety. Permission is also granted to charge for the cost of copying.

Unless otherwise indicated, all Scripture quotations are taken from the New King James Version ®, Copyright © 1979, 1980, 1982 by Thomas Nelson, Inc. Used by permission. All rights reserved.

TABLE OF CONTENTS

INTRODUCTION 1

GENESIS: THE ELECTION OF GOD 3

EXODUS: THE PURPOSE OF THE REDEMPTION OF GOD 5

LEVITICUS: THE HOLINESS OF GOD 7

NUMBERS: THE FAITHFULNESS OF GOD 9

DEUTERONOMY: OBEDIENCE TO GOD 11

JOSHUA: POSSESSION OF THE LAND 13

JUDGES: DEPARTURE FROM THE LORD 15

RUTH: REDEMPTION BY A KINSMAN 17

1 SAMUEL: THE ESTABLISHMENT OF THE KINGDOM 19

2 SAMUEL: THE EXPANSION OF THE KINGDOM 21

1 KINGS: THE DIVISION OF THE KINGDOM 23

2 KINGS: THE DESTRUCTION OF THE KINGDOM 25

1 CHRONICLES: PREPARING FOR THE TEMPLE 27

2 CHRONICLES: BUILDING OF THE TEMPLE 29

EZRA: RESTORATION 31

NEHEMIAH: CONTINUAL RESTORATION 33

ESTHER: PROVIDENCE OF GOD 35

JOB: THE SUFFERING OF THE RIGHTEOUS 37

PSALMS: PRAISE 39

PROVERBS: WISDOM 41

ECCLESIASTES: THE FUTILITY OF LIFE 43

SONG OF SOLOMON: ROMANTIC LOVE 45

ISAIAH: THE SALVATION OF GOD 47

JEREMIAH: THE JUDGMENT OF GOD 49

LAMENTATIONS: THE LAMENT 51

EZEKIEL: THE GLORY OF GOD 53

DANIEL: THE SOVEREIGNTY OF GOD 55

HOSEA: THE LOVE OF GOD 57

JOEL: THE DAY OF THE LORD 59

AMOS: THE JUDGMENT OF GOD 61

OBADIAH: THE JUDGMENT OF EDOM 63

JONAH: THE GRACE OF GOD 65

MICAH: SUMMONS TO JUDGMENT	67
NAHUM: THE JUDGMENT ON NINEVEH	69
HABAKKUK: THE RIGHTEOUSNESS OF GOD	71
ZEPHANIAH: THE DAY OF THE LORD	73
HAGGAI: THE REBUILDING OF THE TEMPLE	75
ZECHARIAH: THE FUTURE OF JERUSALEM	77
MALACHI: THE CHARGES OF GOD	79
MATTHEW: THE KINGSHIP OF JESUS CHRIST	81
MARK: THE SERVANTHOOD OF JESUS CHRIST	83
LUKE: THE HUMANITY OF JESUS CHRIST	85
JOHN: THE DEITY OF JESUS CHRIST	87
ACTS: THE SPREAD OF CHRISTIANITY	89
ROMANS: THE RIGHTEOUSNESS OF GOD	91
1 CORINTHIANS: DISORDERS IN THE CHURCH	93
2 CORINTHIANS: THE TRUE MINISTRY	95
GALATIANS: FREEDOM FROM THE MOSAIC LAW	97
EPHESIANS: THE CALLING OF THE BELIEVER	99
PHILIPPIANS: LIVING WORTHY OF THE GOSPEL	101
COLOSSIANS: THE SUFFICIENCY OF CHRIST	103
1 THESSALONIANS: THE BOOK OF SANCTIFICATION	105
2 THESSALONIANS: CORRECTION OF PROPHECY	107
1 TIMOTHY: CONDUCT IN THE CHURCH	109
2 TIMOTHY: THE MINISTRY OF THE WORD	111
TITUS: ORDER IN THE CHURCH	113
PHILEMON: AN EXAMPLE OF LOVE	115
HEBREWS: THE SUPERIORITY OF CHRIST	117
JAMES: HANDLING TRIALS	119
1 PETER: THE SALVATION OF THE SOUL	121
2 PETER: THE SECOND COMING OF CHRIST	123
1 JOHN: FELLOWSHIP WITH THE TRUE GOD	125
2 JOHN: THE TRUTH OF GOD	127
3 JOHN: THE PRACTICE OF LOVE	129
JUDE: FALSE TEACHERS	131
REVELATION: JUDGMENT BY JESUS CHRIST	133
THE OLD TESTAMENT	135
THE NEW TESTAMENT	136

INTRODUCTION

The Bible is the Word of God. "All Scripture is given by inspiration of God" (2 Tim. 3:16). The human authors of Scripture wrote, "as they were moved by the Holy Spirit" (2 Pet. 1:21). Thus, "no prophecy of scripture is of any private interpretation" (2 Pet. 1:20). Prophets who wrote Scripture were not writing their interpretation of events. Instead, "holy men of God" (2 Pet. 1:21) wrote God's message as the Holy Spirit moved them.

Books The Bible is not a single volume written by one human author at one particular time. It is a library of books written by numerous authors at different times over about 1500 years to address specific situations. Notice: *God* used *human authors* to record *His message* to people in *specific situations.*

Profitable The fact that God delivered His message to address specific situations does not mean that the spiritual truths involved were limited to that situation. All Scripture is profitable "for doctrine (teaching), for reproof, for correction, for instruction in righteousness" (2 Tim. 3:16). Two of these are negative (reproof and correction) and two are positive (teaching and instruction). Scripture is designed to inform believers about what needs to be taken out of their lives (reproof and correction) and what needs to be put into their lives (teaching and instruction). For example, the Bible is full of biographical material. The lives of the men and women in the Bible "become our examples" (1 Cor. 10:6). God uses their lives to teach believers what they should and should not do. So, while God's messages originally addressed specific situations, the spiritual truths apply to believers today. "For whatever things were written before were written for our learning" (Rom. 15:4). Therefore, although God moved men to write the books of the Bible many years ago, they contain spiritual truths that apply to believers today.

Understanding a Book of the Bible

Subject Since God chose to communicate through books, the nature of a book needs to be understood. As is the case in all well-written books, each book of the Bible has an overall **subject**. Some biblical books state the subject of the book at the beginning of the book. For example, the subject of Ecclesiastes is "Vanity of vanity all is vanity" (Eccl. 1:2). The subject of 1 John is "fellowship" (1 Jn. 1:4). The subject of the book of Revelation is the "revelation of Jesus Christ (Rev. 1:1). Not all biblical books, however, state the subject. When the subject is not stated, it has to be determined by an analysis of the book's content.

Structure The nature of a book is the **development of a subject**. Some biblical books state the development of the book's subject by giving an outline of the book. For example, the book of Revelation contains the book's outline in Revelation 1:19, which says, "Write the things which you have seen, and the things which are, and the things which will take place after this." The book of Acts states a geographical outline of the book in Acts 1:8, which says, "But you shall receive power when the Holy Spirit has come upon you, and you shall be witnesses to Me in Jerusalem, and in all Judea and Samaria, and to the end of the earth." (Acts 1:8 is a geographical outline of the book, not necessarily an outline of the book's subject.)

Some biblical books contain an outline of the book within the book by repeating a phrase. The outline of the book of Genesis is the repeated phrase "this is the generation of." The outline of the book of Malachi is a series of God's accusations against Israel: 1) You have doubted My love (Mal. 1:2). 2) You have despised My name (Mal. 1:6), etc. Most biblical books, however, do not contain an outline of the book. When the development of the book's subject is not indicated, the development of the book's subject has to be determined by analyzing the book's content.

Situation Virtually all biblical books were written to address a **specific situation**. The specific situation involves *who* wrote the book, to *whom* it was written, and *why* the author wrote on that subject to the original recipient. In other words, the specific situation involves the *author*, including the date he wrote, the *recipients*, including details of their situation, and the *purpose*. The available information concerning the specific situation is determined by analyzing the book's content.

Summary The combination of the subject and the development of the subject in a sentence is the book's **message**. Each book of the Bible contains **spiritual truth** that is profitable. Jesus said God's Word is truth and it is that truth that sanctifies believers (Jn. 17:7). In other words, to be sanctified (set apart) and grow to spiritual maturity, believers must practice the spiritual truth in the Word of God. Each biblical book consists of one overall spiritual truth and other spiritual truths.

Significant Verses Each book of the Bible contains **significant verses**. Some verses help explain the book it is in; some are pertinent to understanding the Bible, and some state profitable spiritual truth.

Understanding this Book

The **subject** of each biblical book is given in the title and is repeated in the first line of the first paragraph. The book's **structure** (the development of the subject) is stated in the second paragraph and then given in outline form. After the outline, the **situation** is explained by giving the *author* (including the date), *recipients* (including details), and *purpose*. The summary statement contains the overall **message** of the book, followed by the **overall spiritual truth** of the book. **Significant verses** are on the second page. The references to the verses that contain profitable spiritual truths are underlined. You may want to add other verses that are significant to you.

May the Lord use this material to help you understand each of the 66 books in the Bible and the spiritual truths they contain so that you may grow to Christlike spiritual maturity.

G. Michael Cocoris
Santa Monica, California

PS The overall spiritual truth of the Bible is that the sovereign, holy, loving God, who created the universe, desires to have a relationship with you. Spiritual truths concerning Him, you, and the relationship between the two of you are of the utmost importance.

GENESIS: THE ELECTION OF GOD

Subject The subject of Genesis is the election of God. God chose people for a purpose.

Structure The phrase "These are the generations of" occurs eleven times (2:4; 5:1; 6:9; 10:1; 11:10, 27; 25:12, 19; 36:1, 9; 37:2). In Genesis 5:1, it appears as "This is the book of the genealogy of," indicating that these phrases designate written records. These 11 phrases are the stories of individuals such as Adam, Noah, the sons of Noah, Shem, Terah (father of Abraham), Ishmael, Isaac, Esau (twice), and Jacob. These divisions of the book can be summarized in two main points.

I. God's Election in the Primeval History of Humanity	1:1-11:26
A. The Creation of the Earth	1:1-2:3
B. The Development of Sin	2:4-6:8
C. The Judgment of the Flood	6:9-9:29
D. The Descendants of Noah	10:1-11:26
II. God's Election in the Patriarchal History of Israel	11:27-50:26
A. The Story of Abraham	11:27-25:11
B. The Story of Isaac	25:12-26:35
C. The Story of Jacob	27:1-37:1
D. The Story of Joseph	37:2-50:26

Author Moses probably wrote Genesis in 1447 BC, shortly after the Exodus. The events of Genesis ended in 1806 BC, hundreds of years before the Exodus. How did Moses know about what happened hundreds of years before he wrote? The repeated phrase "These are the generations of" indicates that Moses used written records to write (edit) Genesis, which means the material was written years before by people who were living at the time. The Lord had Moses use these written records in writing His Word. (Inspiration is the *recording* of truth, either revealed by God, based on other written material, or based on the author's experience.)

Recipients The recipients were the complaining Israelites (the Exodus generation; see "For you have brought us out into this wilderness to kill this whole assembly with hunger" in Ex. 16:3 and "Why *is* it you have brought us up out of Egypt, to kill us and our children and our livestock with thirst?" in Ex. 17:3). They had questions, such as "Why is Moses leading us out of Egypt? Where is he taking us? Why is he taking us there?"

Purpose Thus, the purpose of Genesis is to inform the Exodus generation about God's promises to Abraham, Isaac, and Jacob and to explain how they got to Egypt.

Summary: The overall message of Genesis is God, the Creator, chose the Patriarchs and their descendants to give them the land of Canaan and bless the world through them, but they ended up in Egypt.

The overall spiritual truth of Genesis is that God, the Creator, elects, justifies, and blesses. Justification is by faith, that is, faith is counted for righteousness (15:6).

Genesis 1:1 "In the beginning God created the heavens and the earth."

Genesis 1:27 "So God created man in His own image; in the image of God He created him: male and female He created them."

Genesis 2:24 "Therefore a man shall leave his father and mother and be joined to his wife, and they shall become one flesh.

Genesis 3:1 "He [the serpent] said to the woman, 'Has God indeed said, 'You shall not eat of every tree in the garden?'"

Genesis 3:6 "So when the woman saw that the tree was good for food, that it was pleasant to the eye, and a tree desirable to make one wise, she took of its fruit and ate. She also gave her husband with her, and he ate."

Genesis 3:12 Adam told the Lord, "The woman whom you gave to be with me, she gave me the tree, and I ate."

Genesis 3:16 "The Lord told the serpent, "I will put enmity between you and the woman, and between your seed and her Seed; He shall bruise your head, and you shall bruise His heel."

Genesis 3:23 "The Lord God sent him out of the garden of Eden."

Genesis 6:8 "Noah found grace in the eyes of the Lord."

Genesis 12:1-3 "Now the LORD had said to Abram: 'Get out of your country, From your family And from your father's house, To a land that I will show you. I will make you a great nation; I will bless you And make your name great; And you shall be a blessing. I will bless those who bless you, And I will curse him who curses you; and in you, all the families of the earth shall be blessed.'" This passage is the key to the Bible, at least the Old Testament. God chose Abraham and his descendants, that is, the Jews, to bless the world. He used them to give us the Scripture and the Messiah. The spiritual truth here is that God blesses us so we can bless others.

Genesis 15:6 "And he believed in the LORD, and He accounted it to him for righteousness."

Genesis 18:14 When Sarah, who was past childbearing age, laughed within herself because she was told she would have a child, the Lord asked Abraham, "Is anything too hard for the Lord?"

Genesis 18:17-19 "And the LORD said, 'Shall I hide from Abraham what I am doing, since Abraham shall surely become a great and mighty nation, and all the nations of the earth shall be blessed in him? For I have known him, in order that he may command his children and his household after him, that they keep the way of the LORD, to do righteousness and justice, that the LORD may bring to Abraham what He has spoken to him.'"

Genesis 18:25 In pleading with the Lord to spare Sodom and Gomorrah, Abraham asked, "Shall not the judge of all the earth do right?"

Genesis 49:10 "The scepter shall not depart from Judah, nor a lawgiver from between his feet, until Shiloh comes; and to Him *shall be* the obedience of the people."

Genesis 50:20 Joseph said to his brothers who sold him into slavery, "You meant evil against me, but God meant it for good, in order to bring it about as it is this day, to save many people alive."

The spiritual lessons of Genesis include God made human beings in His image (Gen. 1:27) and when they disobeyed God, He sent them out of the Garden of Eden (Gen. 3:24). Nevertheless, God promised to send One who would destroy the serpent (Gen. 3:15). In the meantime, some found the *grace* of God (Gen. 6:8) and those who believed in the Lord were counted righteous (Gen. 15:6). Disobedient, unrighteous humans can have a relationship with God by grace through faith. Those who are blessed are to bless others (Gen. 12:1-3).

EXODUS: THE PURPOSE OF THE REDEMPTION OF GOD

Subject The subject of Exodus is not just redemption but the purpose of redemption.

Structure In Exodus, the Israelites were in Egypt, in the wilderness, and at Sinai, where God made a covenant with them, including giving them the Law and the Tabernacle.

I. God Redeemed Israel from Egypt	1:1-18:27
A. God Prepared a Leader	1:1-6:30
B. God Challenged the Egyptians	7:1-12:36
C. God Redeemed Israel from Egypt	12:37-18:27
II. God Made a Covenant with Israel	19:1-24:18
A. The Acceptance of the Covenant	19:1-25
B. The Book of the Covenant	20:1-23:33
C. The Ratification of the Covenant	24:1-18
III. God Established the Tabernacle	25:1-40:38
D. The Plan for the Tabernacle	25:1-31:18
E. The Breaking of the Covenant	32:1-34:35
F. The Construction of the Tabernacle	35:1-40:38

Author Moses wrote Exodus (17:14; 24:4-7; 34:27), probably about 1446 BC.

Recipients The recipients were the Exodus generation Israelites. These newly redeemed people and future generations needed a reminder of how God had redeemed them by blood and power, given them His Law, and made provision to dwell among them.

Purpose The purpose of Exodus is to remind the Exodus generation that God redeemed Israel from Egypt so He could give them His Law and His presence.

Summary: The overall message of the Exodus is that God redeemed Israel so He could make a covenant with them, give them His Law, and dwell among them.

The overall spiritual truth of Exodus is that God redeems people so He can give them His Word and be with them.

Exodus 20:1-17 This is a summary of the 10 Commandments.

> "You shall have no other gods before Me.
> "You shall not make for yourself a carved image.
> "You shall not take the name of the LORD your God in vain.
> "Remember the Sabbath day, to keep it holy.
> "Honor your father and your mother.
> "You shall not murder.
> "You shall not commit adultery.
> "You shall not steal.
> "You shall not covet … anything that *is* your neighbor's."

Exodus 34:6-7 When Moses asked the Lord to show him His glory (Exodus 33:18), "The LORD passed before him and proclaimed, 'The LORD, the LORD God, merciful and gracious, longsuffering, and abounding in goodness and truth, keeping mercy for thousands, forgiving iniquity and transgression and sin, by no means clearing *the guilty,* visiting the iniquity of the fathers upon the children and the children's children to the third and the fourth generation.'"

This list of God's characteristics consists basically of two attributes: grace (merciful, gracious, long-suffering, goodness, forgiveness) and truth (truth, justice). The Old Testament says, "God is holy" (Lev. 11:44) and the New Testament says, "God is love" (1 Jn. 4:8). God's children are to be like Him (Lev. 11:45; 1 Pet. 1:15).

These two primary attributes of God are repeatedly emphasized throughout Scripture using several different terms, such as righteousness, justice, and truth on the one hand and love, grace, and mercy on the other.

LEVITICUS: THE HOLINESS OF GOD

Subject The subject of Leviticus is the holiness of God (11:44).

Structure Leviticus does not have a "literary" structure. The closest thing to it is the repetition of the phrase, "And the Lord said to." That phrase occurs 33 times (1:1; 8:1; 11:1; 12:1; 13:1; 14:1; 15:1; 16:1; 17:1; 18:1; 19:1; 20:1; etc.). The book consists of ceremonial and moral laws.

I. Ceremonial Laws for Israel's Holiness   1:1-16:34
    A. The Sacrifices   1:1-7:38
    B. The Priesthood   8:1-10:20
    C. Clean and Unclean   11:1-15:33
    D. Day of Atonement   16:1-34
II. Moral Laws for Israel's Holiness   17:1-27:34
    A. Concerning the People   17:1-20:27
    B. Concerning the Priest   21:1-22:33
    C. Concerning the Feast   23:1-24:23
    D. Concerning the Land   25:1-27:34

Author Moses wrote Leviticus (1:1). The new calendar of Israel began with the first Passover (Ex. 12:1-2). The Tabernacle was completed exactly one year later (Ex. 40:17). According to Leviticus 1:1, the book of Leviticus picks up the story at that point and takes place in the first month of the second year (25:1; 26:46; 27:34). The book of Numbers opens at the beginning of the second month (Num. 1). Therefore, Leviticus takes place in one month. The book was written after the children of Israel camped at Sinai. Since the Exodus occurred in 1447, this book was probably written by Moses in 1446 BC.

Recipients The recipients were the Exodus generation Israelites. This newly redeemed generation needed instruction on how to relate to the Lord morally and ceremonially (spiritually).

Purpose The purpose of Leviticus is to instruct the Exodus generation on how to perform the rituals connected with the Tabernacle and how to obey ceremonial and moral laws that separated them to the Lord so they could have fellowship with Him.

Summary: The overall message of Leviticus is God gave ceremonial and moral laws to Israel so that they might be set apart (sanctified) to Him for fellowship.

The overall spiritual truth of Leviticus is God is holy and He desires His children to be holy (11:45). The Hebrew word "holy" means "to separate or set apart."

Leviticus 11:44 "For I am the Lord your God. You shall therefore consecrate yourself and you shall be holy; for I am holy."

Leviticus 19:2 "You should be holy, for I the Lord your God am holy."

Leviticus 19:18 "You shall not take vengeance, nor bear any grudge against the children of your people, you shall love your neighbor as yourself: I am the Lord."

NUMBERS: THE FAITHFULNESS OF GOD

Subject The subject of Numbers is the faithfulness of God.

Structure Numbers is organized under two numberings of the children of Israel, the Exodus generation and the second generation.

I. God Faithfully Prepares Israel for Departure	1:1-10:10
A. Numbering of the People	1:1-4:9
B. Spiritual Organization of the People	5:1-6:27
C. Closing Events at Sinai	7:1-9:14
D. Signal for March	9:15-10:10
II. God Faithfully Disciplines Israel	10:11-25:18
A. Sinai to Kadesh-Barnea—unbelief	10:11-14:45
B. Kadesh-Barnea to Moab—wandering	15:1-25:18
III. God Faithfully Prepares the Second Generation	26:1-36:13
A. Numbering of the People	26:1-65
B. Laws	27:1-30:16
C. Allotment of the Land	31:1-32:42
D. Recapitulation	33:1-56
E. More Laws	34:1-36:13

Author Moses wrote Numbers (1:1). Numbers picks up where Leviticus leaves off. It records the last 19 days at Mt. Sinai (1:1; 10:11). It reveals Israel's journey from Sinai to Kadesh-Barnea and traces Israel's trip through the various places in the wilderness and finally to the Plain of Moab across the Jordan River from Jericho. The book covers 38 years and nine months. The date is approximately 40 years after the Exodus. Therefore, Moses wrote Numbers somewhere around 1407 BC.

Recipients The original recipients were the second-generation Israelites. The second and the following generations needed a reminder of the consequences of unbelief and the faithfulness of God.

Purpose The purpose of Numbers is to teach God's faithfulness and what unbelief will do (Heb. 3:15-19).

Summary: The overall message of Numbers is God faithfully prepared Israel for entrance into the land, but because of unbelief, they disobeyed, so He disciplined the disobedient and, faithful to His covenant, He prepared a second generation to inherit the land.

The overall spiritual truth of Numbers is God is faithful to fulfill all His promises, including disciplining the disobedient.

Israel's Complaints in the Wilderness

Ex. 17:1-7	lack of water
Num 11:1-3	hardships of desert life
Nu 11:4-35	lack of meat
Nu 14:1-35	size of those living in the land
Nu 16:1-35	authority of Moses and Aaron
Nu 16:41-50	killing Korah & rebels
Num 20:1-13	lack of water
Num 21:4-9	The manna & being in the desert

<u>Numbers 6:24-26</u> "The LORD bless you and keep you; the LORD make His face shine upon you, and be gracious to you; the LORD lift up His countenance upon you, And give you peace."

Numbers 11:1 "Now *when* the people complained, it displeased the LORD; for the LORD heard *it,* and His anger was aroused. So the fire of the LORD burned among them and consumed *some* in the outskirts of the camp."

Numbers 11:4-6 "Now the mixed multitude who were among them yielded to intense craving; so the children of Israel also wept again and said: 'Who will give us meat to eat? We remember the fish which we ate freely in Egypt, the cucumbers, the melons, the leeks, the onions, and the garlic; but now our whole being *is* dried up; *there is* nothing at all except this manna *before* our eyes!'" (11:4-6).

Numbers 11:10-11 "Then Moses heard the people weeping throughout their families, everyone at the door of his tent; and the anger of the LORD was greatly aroused; Moses also was displeased. So Moses said to the LORD, 'Why have You afflicted Your servant? And why have I not found favor in Your sight, that You have laid the burden of all these people on me?'"

When the people complained about not having meat to eat and Moses complained about the people complaining, the Lord taught Moses to delegate and supernaturally gave the people a month's supply of meat that made them so sick, many died. *Beware of complaining.*

Numbers 12:1 "Then Miriam and Aaron spoke against Moses because of the Ethiopian woman whom he had married; for he had married an Ethiopian woman."

Numbers 12:9-10 "So the anger of the Lord was aroused against them and He departed. And when the cloud departed from above the tabernacle, suddenly Miriam *became* leprous, as *white as* snow. Then Aaron turned toward Miriam, and there she was, a leper."

When Miriam and Aaron criticize Moses, the Lord punished Miriam with leprosy and healed her as a result of the intercession of Moses. *Beware of criticizing.*

Numbers 14:2-3 "And all the children of Israel complained against Moses and Aaron, and the whole congregation said to them, 'If only we had died in the land of Egypt! Or if only we had died in this wilderness!' Why has the LORD brought us to this land to fall by the sword, that our wives and children should become victims? Would it not be better for us to return to Egypt?'"

Numbers 14:11-12 When the children of Israel refused to enter the promised land, "the LORD said to Moses: 'How long will these people reject Me? And how long will they not believe Me, with all the signs which I have performed among them? 1 will strike them with the pestilence and disinherit them, and I will make of you a nation greater and mightier than they.'" *Beware of unbelief.*

Numbers 12:6 The Lord describes the nature of a prophet, saying, "If there is a prophet among you, I, the Lord, make Myself known to him in a vision; I speak to him in a dream."

DEUTERONOMY: OBEDIENCE TO GOD

Subject The subject of Deuteronomy is obedience to God.

Structure Deuteronomy is the record of what Moses said to the people in the Plain of Moab (1:1; 5:1; 27:1; 29:1; 31:1; 31:30; 33:1; 34:1). Several arrangements have been suggested. A common way to view Deuteronomy is to see it as a series of sermons.

I. First Sermon: The Historical Appeal for Obedience	1:1-4:49
A. Wilderness Journey	1:1-3:29
B. Exhortation to Obedience	4:1-49
II. Second Sermon: The Legal Basis for Obedience	5:1-26:19
A. The Basic Commandment	5:1-11:32
B. Specific Legislation	12:1-26:19
III. Third Sermon: A Prophetical Exhortation for Obedience	27:1-30:20
A. Covenant Renewal Commanded	27:1-26
B. Blessing and Cursing	28:1-68
C. A Concluding Charge	29:1-30:20
IV. Transitional Details	31:1-34:12
A. Joshua and Law	31:1-30
B. Song of Moses	32:1-52
C. Blessing of Moses	33:1-29
D. Death of Moses	34:1-12

Author Moses wrote Deuteronomy (1:1). Deuteronomy takes place on the Plain of Moab, due east of Jericho, across the Jordan River (1:1, 29:1), and covers only about one month. (*cf.* 1:3, 34:8 with Josh. 5:6-12). It was written at the end of the 40 years in the wilderness. Thus, it was written by Moses in about 1407 BC.

Recipients The original recipients were the second generation of Israelites. The generation and the generations to follow needed a reminder of the importance of obeying the Lord.

Purpose The purpose of Deuteronomy is for Moses to address Israel before he died and they entered the land (1:1; 3:5). He urges the people to obey the Lord (26:16-19). If they did so, they would be blessed. If they didn't, they would be cursed (chs. 27-30, esp. 30:11-18). He also needed to settle transitional details before he died,

Summary: The overall message of Deuteronomy is God blesses those who obey Him and curses those who disobey Him.

The overall spiritual truth of Deuteronomy is God blesses the obedient and disciplines the disobedient. Obedience is the condition for blessing.

Deuteronomy 6:4-9 "Hear, O Israel: the Lord our God, the Lord is one! You shall love the Lord your God with all your heart with all your soul of all yours bring. And these words which I command you today shall be in your heart. You shall teach them diligently to your children and shall talk of them when you sit in your house, when you walk by the way, when you live down, and when you rise up. You shall bind them as signs in your hand and they shall be as frontlets between your eyes. You shall write them on the doorpost of your house and on the gates."

Deuteronomy 18:10-11 "There shall not be found among you *anyone* who makes his son or his daughter pass through the fire, *or one* who practices witchcraft, *or* a soothsayer, or one who interprets omens, or a sorcerer, or one who conjures spells, or a medium, or a spiritist, or one who calls up the dead."

Deuteronomy 18:15 "The LORD your God will raise up for you a Prophet like me from your midst, from your brethren. Him you shall hear."

Deuteronomy 29:29 "The secret things belong to the Lord our God, but those things which are revealed belong to us and to our children forever, that we may do all the words of this law."

Satan tempts Jesus three times. All three times, Jesus responded by quoting Scripture. In all three cases, He quoted Deuteronomy.

Deuteronomy 8:3 "So He humbled you, allowed you to hunger, and fed you with manna which you did not know nor did your fathers know, that He might make you know that man shall not live by bread alone but man shall live by every word that proceeds from the mouth of the Lord."

Deuteronomy 6:16 "You shall not tempt the Lord your God as you tempted Him in Massah."

Deuteronomy 6:13 "You shall fear the Lord your God and serve him and shall take oaths in His name."

In Genesis, a sovereign God elects. In Exodus, a powerful God redeems. In Leviticus, a holy God sanctifies. In Numbers, a faithful God disciplines. In Deuteronomy, a gracious God instructs.

JOSHUA: POSSESSION OF THE LAND

Subject The subject of Joshua is the possession of the land (1:11).

Structure Joshua records the conquest of the land of Canaan. Geography is one of the unifying factors of the book.

I. Entering the Land to Possess it	1:1-5:15
A. The Charge to Joshua	1:1-18
B. The Commissioning of the Spies	2:1-24
C. The Crossing of the Jordan	3:1-17
D. The Construction of the Memorial	4:1-24
E. The Consecration of the Israelites	5:1-15
II. Conquering the Land to Possess it	6:1-12:24
A. The Central Campaign	6:1-8:35
B. The Southern Campaign	9:1-10:43
C. The Northern Campaign	11:1-5
D. The Review of the Victories	11:6-12:24
III. The Division of the Land to Possess it	13:1-21:45
A. The Division of the Land	13:1-19:51
B. The Cities of Refuge	20:1-9
C. The Cities of the Levites	21:1-45
IV. Appendix	22:1-24:33
A. The Dismissal of the Eastern Tribes	22:1-34
B. The Farewell of Joshua	23:1-24:33

Author The author of Joshua is anonymous. Joshua wrote at least parts of the book (see "we" and "us" in 5:1, 6; 18:9; 24:26). Three small portions, however, must have been added after his death: 1) Othniel's capture of Kirjath-Sepher (5:13-19; Judges 1:9-15), 2) Dan's migration to the north (19:47; Judges 18:27-29) and 3) Joshua's death and burial (24:29-33). Eleazar, the priest, and his son, Phinehas (24:33), may have inserted these in the time of Judges. The Exodus took place in 1447 BC. The conquest began 40 years later, in 1407 BC. The conquest was completed in 7 years (14:7, 10). Thus, Joshua was written around 1400 BC or possibly shortly after that.

Recipients The original recipients were the second-generation Israelites. They are the ones who possess the land. The word "possession" occurs no less than 22 times. There is a difference between ownership and possession. Israel's ownership over the land was unconditional (Gen. 15:7-21, etc.), but her possession of the land was conditional (Deut. 29:9, 30:20). God told Joshua, "You got it" (1:2-3); now "go get it" (1:5-6).

Purpose The purpose of Joshua is to document how God led the Israelites into the land, how they conquered it, and how it was divided among them.

Summary: The overall message of Joshua is God had led the second generation into the land, enabled them to conquer it, and divided it among them.

The overall spiritual message of Joshua is when God's people trust Him and obey Him, they possess their possessions. We need to trust the Lord and obey His Word so that we can possess our God-given possessions.

Joshua 1:7-9 "Only be strong and very courageous, that you may observe to do according to all the law which Moses my servant commanded you; do not turn from it to the right hand or to the left, you may prosper wherever you go. This book of the law shall not depart out of your mouth, but you shall meditate in it day and night that you may observe to do according to all that is written in it. For then you will make your way prosperous and then you will have good success. Have I not commanded you? Be strong and of good courage; do not be afraid, nor be dismayed, for the Lord your God is with you wherever you go."

Joshua 11:15 "As the Lord had commanded Moses, His servant, so Moses commanded Joshua, and so Joshua did. He left nothing undone of all that the Lord had commanded Moses."

Joshua 24:15 "Choose for yourselves this day whom you will serve … But as for me and my house, we will serve the Lord."

JUDGES: DEPARTURE FROM THE LORD

Subject The subject of Judges is departure from the Lord.

Structure "The children of Israel did evil in the sight of the Lord" appears six times (3:7, 3:12; 4:1; 6:12; 10:6; 13:1). "In those days, there was no king in Israel; everyone did what was right in his own eyes" appears four times (17:6; 21:25; 18:1; 19:1).

I.	Introduction: Israel Departed from the Lord	1:1-3:6
	A. Politically: Failure to Completely Conquer	1:1-36
	B. Spiritually: Departure, Degeneration, Defeat, Deliverance	2:1-3:6
II.	The Judges: Departure, Defeat, and Delivered by a Judge	3:7-16:31
	A. First Apostasy: conquered by Mesopotamia (Othniel)	3:7-12
	B. Second Apostasy: conquered by Mesopotamia and the Philistines (Ehud and Shamgar)	3:12-31
	C. Third Apostasy: conquered by Jabin (Deborah and Barak)	4:1-5:31
	D. Fourth Apostasy: conquered by Midians (Gideon, Tola, and Jair)	6:1-10:5
	E. Fifth Apostasy: conquered by the Philistines and the Ammonites (Jepthah, Ibzan, and Abdon)	10:6-12:15
	F. Sixth Apostasy: conquered by the Philistines (Samson)	13:1-16:31
III.	Appendix: Departure, Depravity, Desire for a King	17:1-21:25
	A. The Idolatry of Dan	17:1-18:31
	B. The Crime of Benjamin	19:1-21:15

Author The author is anonymous. The Talmud attributes the book to Samuel, who was an author (1 Sam. 10:25). Samuel or one of his prophetic students probably wrote it. Judges was written after Samson's death (16:30; 1051 BC). "In those days there was no king in Israel" (17:6; 21:25; 18:1; 19:1) indicates it was written after the beginning of Saul's reign (1043 BC). Judges 1:21 says that the Jebusites were dwelling in Jerusalem "to this day," which is when David disposed of the Jebusites (2 Sam. 5:5-9; 1004 BC). Thus, Judges was written between 1043 BC and 1004 BC, probably about 1040 BC.

Recipients The original recipients were the Israelites who lived just after the first king was crowned. Judges 2:11-19 explains the book of Judges. The pattern of the period is defection from the Lord, degeneration, defeat, and then deliverance (sin, servitude, supplication, and salvation, meaning deliverance). Defection led to people doing what was right in their own eyes and the need for a king (17:6; 18:1; 19:1; 21:25). When they didn't have a king, everyone did what was right in his own eyes. There was a need for a king to give order and stability to Israel.

Purpose The purpose of Judges is to demonstrate that repeated departure from the Lord resulted in people doing what was right in their own eyes and, therefore, the need for a king.

Summary: The overall message is that departure from the Lord leads to degeneration, defeat and, eventually, the need for a king.

The overall spiritual truth of Judges is that when people depart from the Lord, they do that which is right in their own eyes, which leads to the need for a king.

Judges 2:11, 14, 16 "Then the children of Israel did evil in the sight of the Lord and served Baals; and they forsook the Lord their God of their fathers…. And the anger of the Lord was hot against Israel. So He delivered them into the hands of plunderers who despoiled them….. Nevertheless, the Lord raised up judges who delivered them out of the hand of those who plundered them." Defection from the Lord (sin) leads to degeneration (servitude), but supplication leads to deliverance (salvation).

<u>**Judges 17:6**</u> "In those days there was no king in Israel; everyone did what was right in his own eyes."
Judges 18:1 "In those days there was no king in Israel. And in those days, the tribe of the Danites was seeking an inheritance for itself to dwell in."
Judges 19:1 "And it came to pass in those days when there was no king in Israel."
Judges 21:25 "In those days there was no king in Israel; everyone did what was right in his own eyes."

The chronological notices in the book total of 410 years. That is a problem. First Kings 6:1 says the fourth year of Solomon's reign was 480 years after the Exodus. Israel wandered in the wilderness for 40 years, and the conquest took seven years. There may have also been a gap of a few years between the conquest of the land and the beginning of the first judge. To those figures, forty years for Saul and forty years for David need to be added, plus four years of Solomon's reign. The total of these is at least 131 years (40+7+?+40+40+4 = at least 131), leaving only 349 + years for the period of the Judges (480-131-? = 349 +), but the chronological notices in the book total of 410 years.

The solution to this apparent discrepancy is to conclude that some of the judges ruled contemporaneously, reducing the total length of the period from 410 years to about 350 years. For example, Judges 10:7 clearly implies that Jephthah and Samson ruled simultaneously since one delivered oppressed Israel from the Ammonites and the other from the Philistines. In other words, not all the judges ruled over the *whole* land as our President does the whole nation. Instead, they were like our governors, ruling over smaller areas and, at times, some of them ruled over different areas simultaneously. Thus, the entire period of the Judges was only about 350 years, from about 1390 BC until about 1043 BC, when Saul became King.

RUTH: REDEMPTION BY A KINSMAN

Subject The subject of Ruth is redemption by a kinsman redeemer.

Structure Ruth is almost pure narrative. If there is a literary structure, it revolves around places.

  I.   Ruth follows Naomi to Bethlehem   1:1-22
  II. Ruth gleans in Boaz's Field   2:1-23
  III. Ruth seeks to marry Boaz   3:1-18
  IV. Ruth marries Boaz   4:1-22

Author The author is anonymous. There is not the slightest hint or clue in the book as to who wrote it. The Talmud attributes it to Samuel. Samuel anointed David as king. So he could have written Ruth after he anointed David. Samuel did not live to see David become king. The events of the book took place during the period of the Judges (1:1), which was between 1375 BC and 1043 BC, but the book traces the lineage of Ruth to David (4:17). It does not mention Solomon. So, it was written before David's death. David reigned from 1011 through 971 BC. Samuel could have written Ruth about 1016 or 1015 BC. That means it was written years after the events, which is why the author explains the shoe covenant (4:7-8). By the time the book was written, that custom was no longer practiced in Israel.

Recipients The original recipients were the Israelites who lived about 1015 BC. All that can be said about the recipients of this book is that they were not the people who lived during the period of the Judges, but rather, they were the people who lived during David's day.

Purpose The key to the purpose of Ruth is Ruth 4:17, which says, "Also the neighbor women gave him a name, saying, 'There is a son born to Naomi.' And they called his name Obed. He *is* the father of Jesse, the father of David." Ruth 4:18-22 connects Perez, the son of Judah, with David, who is connected to the tribe of Judah. The line, of course, passes through Boaz, Ruth's husband. So, the purpose of Ruth is to introduce the line of David. Ruth also illustrates redemption by a near-kinsman. Ruth was under the condemnation of the Law from her birth. The Mosaic Law forbade a Moabitess from entering the congregation of the Lord (Deut. 23:3). The Law provided, however, for a near-kinsman to redeem a brother and his inheritance (Lev. 25; Num. 35; Deut. 19, 25).

Summary: The overall message of Ruth is a Moabitess was redeemed by a near kinsman.
The overall spiritual message of Ruth is God redeems by a kinsman.

Ruth 1:16-17 "But Ruth said:

>'Treat me not to leave you or to turn back from following after you;
>for wherever you go, I will go;
>and wherever you lodge, I will live;
>your people shall be my people,
>and your God, my God.
>Where you die, I will die,
>and there I will be buried.
>The Lord so do to me and more also,
>if anything but death parts you and me.'"

Ruth 2:3 "Then she left and went and glean in the field after reapers. And she happened to come to the part of the field the longing to Boaz who was of the family of Elimelech."

Ruth 4:17 "Also the neighbor women gave him a name, saying, 'There is a son born to Naomi.' And they called his name Obed. He *is* the father of Jesse, the father of David."

In Exodus, redemption is by the blood of a lamb. In Ruth, redemption is by a near-kinsman. Jesus Christ qualifies for both types of redeemers. He is a near-kinsman, the Son of God, and He is the Lamb of God (see Jn. 1:29).

1 SAMUEL: THE ESTABLISHMENT OF THE KINGDOM

Subject The subject of 1 Samuel is the establishment of the kingdom.

Structure The literary structure of 1 Samuel is people, namely Samuel, Saul, and David (1:1; 9:1; 16:1).

I. Samuel: Transition of Leadership from Eli to Samuel	1:1-8:22
A. His birth and boyhood	1:1-2:10
B. Eli's rejection and Samuel's call	2:11-3:21
C. The Philistines and the Ark	4:1-7:17
D. Israel's Demand for a King.	8:1-22
II. Saul: Establishment of the Kingdom under Saul	9:1-15:35
A. Received and reigning	9:1-12:25
B. Rebuilding and rejected	13:1-15:35
III. David: Establishment of the Kingdom under David	16:1-31:13
A. David's rise as a shepherd	16:1-17:58
B. David's service as a courtier	18:1-19:24
C. David's training as a fugitive	20:1-31:13

Author The author is anonymous. First and 2 Samuel were originally one book. Jewish tradition says Samuel wrote it. He may have written 1 Samuel 1-24, but he did not write the remainder of 1 Samuel or 2 Samuel because his death is recorded in 1 Samuel 25:1. First Chronicles 29:29 refers to the "book of Samuel, the seer," and "the book of Nathan, the prophet," and "the book of Gad, the seer." Those three men were said to have recorded David's acts from the first to the last. Perhaps all three contributed to 1 and 2 Samuel. First Samuel covers 94 years from Samuel's birth to Saul's death (about 1105-1011 BC) and 2 Samuel extends to the end of the life of David. In 1 Samuel 27:6, a reference is made to the divided kingdom, which didn't exist until after the death of Solomon. So, the date is probably about 925 BC.

Recipients The original recipients were the Israelites who lived at the time. They and the following generations in Israel needed to know about the establishment of the kingdom.

Purpose The purpose is to remind the nation of Israel how the kingdom came to be established and teach them spiritual truths.

Summary: The overall message of 1 Samuel is God established a kingdom in Israel.

The overall spiritual truth of 1 Samuel is in God's kingdom, He ruled through people using prophets to reveal His will.

First Samuel covers the transition of leadership in Israel from the Judges to the Kings, from a theocracy to a monarchy.

1 Samuel 2:6-8 in her prayer, Hannah said, "The Lord kills and makes alive; He brings down to the grave and He brings up. The Lord makes poor and makes rich; He brings low and he lifts up. He raises the poor from the dust and lifts the beggar from the ash, to set them among princes and make them inherit the throne of glory."

1 Samuel 12:23 Saul said to the people, "Moreover, as for me, far be it from me that I should sin against the Lord in ceasing to pray for you; but I will teach you the good and right way."

1 Samuel 15:22-23 "So Samuel said [to Saul]: 'Has the LORD *as great* delight in burnt offerings and sacrifices, As in obeying the voice of the LORD? Behold, to obey is better than sacrifice, *And* to heed than the fat of rams. For rebellion *is as* the sin of witchcraft, And stubbornness *is as* iniquity and idolatry. Because you have rejected the word of the LORD, He also has rejected you from *being* king.'"

1 Samuel 17:45 "Then David said to the Philistine [Goliath], 'You come to me with the sword, with the spear, and with a javelin. But I come to you in the name of the Lord of host, the God of armies of Israel, whom you have defiled."

2 SAMUEL: THE EXPANSION OF THE KINGDOM

Subject The subject of 2 Samuel is the consolidation and expansion of the kingdom.

Structure The literary structure of 2 Samuel is the story of David. The book is a narrative of one story or event after another. The phrase "and it came to pass" occurs several times (1:1; 2:1; 7:1; 7:4; 8:1; 10:1; 11:1; 11:14; 13:1; 15:1).

I.	David's Triumphs: The Consolidation of the Kingdom	1:1-10:19
	A. King over Judah Only—at Hebron	1:1-4:12
	B. King over All Israel—at Jerusalem	5:1-10:19
II.	David's Troubles: In the Consolidated Kingdom	11:1-24:25
	A. In His Family	11:1-18:33
	B. In His Nation	19:1-24:25

Author and Recipients Since 1 and 2 Samuel were originally one book, for the author, and original recipients of 2 Samuel, see 1 Samuel.

Purpose The purpose of 2 Samuel is to trace the consolidation and expansion of the kingdom. As 2 Samuel opens, David is made king, but only over Judah. By the end of chapter 4, he is king over all of Israel. With his rule established over the kingdom, David's rule expands to the boundaries originally promised to Abraham. Second Samuel does not end with the expansion of the kingdom. It goes on to tell of David's nose dive. He fell into sin and that sin affected his family and the nation.

Summary: The overall message of 2 Samuel is David, with God's blessing, consolidated and expanded the kingdom, but his sin weakened it.

God wants to use His people to expand His kingdom (rule).

2 Samuel 2:20 concerning the death of Saul and Jonathan, David said, "Tell it not in Gath; proclaim it not in the streets of Ashkelon, lest the daughters of the Philistine rejoice, lest the daughters of the uncircumcised triumph."

2 Samuel 7:16 The Lord told David, "Your house and your kingdom shall be established forever before you. Your throne shall be established forever." This is the Davidic Covenant that is not called a covenant in 2 Samuel, but is called a covenant in Psalm 89:34.

2 Samuel 12:23 Concerning the child of adultery with Bathsheba who died, David said, "But Now he is dead; why should I fast? Can I bring him back again? I shall go to him, but he shall not return to me."

2 Samuel 13:15 "Then Amnon hated her [Tamar] exceedingly so that the hatred with which he hated her *was* greater than the love with which he had loved her. And Amnon said to her, 'Arise, be gone!'"

2 Samuel 15:26 As David was fleeing to Jerusalem, the priest took the ark, perhaps thinking the ark would protect them. David told them to take it back, adding, "If I have found favor in the eyes of the Lord, He will bring me back and show me both it and His dwelling place. But if He Says Thus: 'I Have No Delight In You,' Let Him Do To Me As Seems Good To Him."

2 Samuel 24:24 "Then the king said to Araunah, 'No, but I will surely buy *it* from you for a price; nor will I offer burnt offerings to the LORD my God with that which costs me nothing.' So David bought the threshing floor and the oxen for fifty shekels of silver."

1 KINGS: THE DIVISION OF THE KINGDOM

Subject The subject of 1 Kings is the division of the kingdom.

Structure First Kings is the story of Solomon and the kings who ruled after the division of the kingdom.

I.	The United Kingdom (Reign of Solomon)	1:1-11:43
	A. Solomon's Rule Established	1:1-4:34
	B. Solomon's Temple and Palace Built	5:1-8:66
	C. Solomon's Fame and Glory	9:1-10:29
	D. Solomon's Downfall and Death	11:1-43
II.	The Divided Kingdom (Reign of Kings)	12:1-22:53
	A. The Division of the Kingdom	12:1-24
	B. Reign of Jeroboam in Israel	12:25-14:20
	C. Reign of Rehoboam in Judah	14:21-41
	D. Reign of Abijam in Judah	15:1-8
	E. Reign of Asa in Judah	15:9-24
	F. Reign of Nadab in Israel	15:25-31
	G. Reign of Baasha in Israel	15:32-16:7
	H. Reign of Elah in Israel	16:8-14
	I. Reign of Zimri in Israel	16:15-20
	J. Reign of Omri in Israel (Ministry of Elijah)	16:29-22:40
	K. Reign of Jehoshaphat in Judah	22:41-50
	L. Reign of Ahaziah in Israel	22:51-53

Author The author is anonymous. First and 2 Kings were originally one book. The Talmud says Jeremiah wrote it. There are similarities between Kings and Jeremiah. The author used sources (see 1 Kings 11:41; 14:19, 14:29; 15:7), probably Isaiah 36-39 and perhaps an official court record (2 Kings 18:18). First Kings covers about 123 years, from the death of David to the death of Jehoshaphat (971 to 848 BC). Second Kings covers about 266 years, from the reign of Ahaziah to the Babylonian captivity (852 to 586 BC). Furthermore, 2 Kings 25:7 extends to about 26 years beyond the captivity. Some say "to this day" (8:8; 12:19) indicates authorship prior to the Babylonian captivity (586 BC), but 2 Kings 25:27 indicates that the book was written after it. If Kings was written both before and after the Babylonian captivity, it was probably compiled by either Jeremiah or a contemporary of Jeremiah. Thus, the date is ca. 600-570 BC.

Recipients The original recipients were the Israelites in Babylon, including Daniel and Ezekiel.

Purpose The purpose of Kings is to give God's point of view of the reign of the kings from Solomon to Jehoshaphat (Judah) and Ahaziah (Israel). It evaluates the kings of the divided kingdom (11:6; 13:33; 14:22; 15:26, 34; 16:19, 25, 30; 22:52) according to the standard of Jeroboam in Israel (13:33-34; 15:30, 34; 16:3-5; 16:326; etc.).

Summary: The overall message of 1 Kings is that a divided heart in Solomon led to a division in the kingdom.

The overall spiritual truth of 1 Kings is sin leads to decline and division.

1 Kings 2:3 David told Solomon, "And keep the charge of the LORD your God: to walk in His ways, to keep His statutes, His commandments, His judgments, and His testimonies, as it is written in the Law of Moses, that you may prosper in all that you do and wherever you turn."

1 Kings 3:9 "Therefore, give to Your servant an understanding heart to judge Your people, that I may discern between good and evil. For who is able to judge this great people of Yours?"

2 KINGS: THE DESTRUCTION OF THE KINGDOM

Subject The subject of 2 Kings is the destruction of the kingdom.
Structure Second Kings is the story of one king after another.

I.	The Destruction of the Northern Kingdom	1:1-17:41
	A. Reign of Ahaziah in Israel	1:1-18
	B. Reign of Jehoram in Israel (Ministry of Elisha)	2:1-8:15
	C. Reign of Jehoram in Judah	8:16-24
	D. Reign of Ahaziah in Judah	8:25-29
	E. Reign of Jehu in Israel	9:1-10:36
	F. Reign of Athalia in Judah	11:1-16
	G. Reign of Jehoash in Judah	11:17-12:21
	H. Reign of Jehoahaz in Israel	13:1-9
	I. Reign of Jehoash in Israel	13:10-25
	J. Reign of Amaziah in Judah	14:1-22
	K. Reign of Jehoboam II in Israel	14:23-29
	L. Reign of Azariah in Judah	15:1-7
	M. Reign of Zechariah in Israel	15:8-12
	N. Reign of Shallum in Israel	15:13-15
	O. Reign of Menahem in Israel	15:16-22
	P. Reign of Pekohiah in Israel	15:23-26
	Q. Reign of Pekah in Israel	15:27-31
	R. Reign of Jothem in Judah	15:32-38
	S. Reign of Ahaz in Judah	16:1-20
	T. Reign of Hoshea in Israel	17:1-41
II.	The Destruction of the Southern Kingdom	18:1-25:30
	A. Reign of Hezekiah	18:1-20:21
	B. Reign of Manasseh	21:1-18
	C. Reign of Amon	21:19-26
	D. Reign of Josiah	22:1-23:30
	E. Reign of Jehoahaz	23:31-33
	F. Reign of Jehoiachim	23:34-24:7
	G. Reign of Jehoiachin	24:8-16
	H. Reign of Zedekiah	24:17-25:21
	I. Gedaliah, the Puppet Governor	25:22-26
	J. The Release of Jehoiachin in Babylon	25:27-30

Author and Recipients For the author and recipients of 2 Kings, see 1 Kings.
Purpose The decline and collapse of the two kingdoms was due to disobedience.
Summary: The overall message is that habitual disobedience led to the decay, defeat, and destruction of the Northern and Southern Kingdoms in Israel.

The overall spiritual truth is that the spiritual climate of a nation determines its political and economic conditions.

2 Kings 17:39 "But the LORD your God you shall fear; and He will deliver you from the hand of all your enemies."

2 Kings 22:8 "Then Hilkiah the high priest said to Shaphan the scribe, 'I have found the Book of the Law in the house of the LORD.' And Hilkiah gave the book to Shaphan, and he read it."

1 CHRONICLES: PREPARING FOR THE TEMPLE

Subject The subject of 1 Chronicles is preparing for the Temple.

Structure The literary structure of the first eight chapters is the phrase "the sons of" (1:5, 1:28; 2:1; 3:1; 4:1; 5:1; 6:1; 7:1, 7:6; etc.). The structure of the rest is chronological. (See "Now it came to pass" in 17:1; 18:1l; 19:1; etc.).

I. The Preparation of the Temple: The History of Israel	1:1-9:44
A. Adam to Abraham	1:1-27
B. Abraham to Jacob	1:28-54
C. Jacob to David	2:1-55
D. David to Captivity	3:1-24
E. Genealogies of the Twelve Tribes	4:1-8:40
F. Jerusalem's Inhabitants	9:1-34
G. The Family of Saul	9:35-44
II. The Preparation of the Temple: The History of David	10:1-29:30
A. David Becomes King	10-12
B. David Returns the Ark to Jerusalem	13-16
C. David Desires to Build a Temple	17:1-27
D. David Goes to War	18-21
E. David Prepares for the Temple	22-23:1
F. David Organizes the Levites	23:2-26:32
G. David Appoints Civil Leaders	27:1-34
H. David's Final Acts	28-29

Author The author is anonymous. First and 2 Chronicles were originally one book. Jewish tradition says the author was Ezra, the priest. The author used sources. First Chronicles 29:29 lists three sources: 1) the book of Samuel, the seer, 2) the book of Nathan, the prophet, and 3) the book of Gad, the seer. Samuel, Nathan, and Gad probably wrote 1 and 2 Samuel. Does Ezra quote Samuel? "No." The material given in 1 Chronicles is not recorded in 2 Samuel, which means that if Nathan and Gad wrote our Samuel, they also wrote another work, which Ezra quotes. The content of the book extends to after the return of the remnant (1 Chron. 9; also *cf.* 1 Chron. 9 with Neh. 1:21:3-32; 7:45 and 12:26, and Ezra 2:42). Ezra led some of the captives to Jerusalem in 458 BC. So, he probably completed Chronicles between 450-440 BC.

Recipients The recipients of Chronicles were the Israelites who returned from Babylon.

Purpose The purpose of Chronicles is to demonstrate the importance of the Temple in the history of Israel. Yet it is not just the Temple building, that is, the Temple building past or Temple building present, but the Temple meant the presence of God.

Summary: The overall message of 1 Chronicles is that in the history of Israel, God, through David and Solomon, gave His presence to them in a Temple.

The overall spiritual truth of 1 Chronicles is God is present with believers and when they acknowledge Him, things of lasting spiritual value are accomplished.

1 Chronicles 4:9-10 "Now Jabez was more honorable than his brothers, and his mother called his name Jabez, saying, 'Because I bore *him* in pain.' And Jabez called on the God of Israel saying, "Oh, that You would bless me indeed, and enlarge my territory, that Your hand would be with me, and that You would keep *me* from evil, that I may not cause pain!" So God granted him what he requested."

1 Chronicles 12:32 "of the sons of Issachar who had understanding of the times, to know what Israel ought to do."

2 CHRONICLES: BUILDING OF THE TEMPLE

Subject The subject of 2 Chronicles is the building of the Temple.

Structure The structure of 2 chronological is marked by the phrases "Now this," "then this," and "and it came to pass").

I. The Temple in the Reign of Solomon	1:1-9:31
A. Solomon's Inauguration	1:1-17
B. Solomon's Temple	2:1-7:22
C. Solomon's Fame	8:1-9:28
D. Solomon's Death	9:29-31
II. The Temple During the Reigns of The Kings of Judah	10:1-36:21
A. Rehoboam	10:1-12:16
B. Abijah	13:1-22
C. Asa	14:1-16:14
D. Jehoshaphat	17:1-20:37
E. Ahaziah	21:1-20
F. Athaliah	22:1-9
G. Joash	22:10-23:15
H. Amaziah	25:1-28
I. Uzziah	26:1-23
J. Jotham	27:1-9
K. Ahaz	28 1-27
L. Hezekiah	29:1-32:33
M. Manasseh	33:1-20
N. Amon	33:21-25
O. Josiah	34:1-35:27
P. Jehoahaz	36:1-4
Q. Jehoiakim	36:5-8
R. Jehoiachin	36:9-10
S. Zedekiah	36:11-21
III. The Decree of Cyrus	36:22-23

Author and Recipients For the author and recipients of 2 Chronicles, see 1 Chronicles. The author used sources (see 9:29; 12:15; 13:22; 16:11; 20:34; 24:27; 26:22; 27:7; 32:33; 33:18).

Purpose The purpose is to demonstrate that when Israel obeyed God, particularly the ordinances of the Temple, they experienced God's blessing.

Summary: The overall message of 2 Chronicles is God blessed those who obeyed His ordinances, especially the Temple worship.

The overall spiritual truth is God is present with believers and when they acknowledge Him, they experience His blessings.

2 Chronicles 7:14 "If My people who are called by My name will humble themselves, and pray and seek My face, and turn from their wicked ways, then I will hear from heaven, and will forgive their sin and heal their land."

Kings centers around the throne, Chronicles around the Temple. Kings highlights the prophets, Chronicles the priests. Thus, Saul and the Northern Kingdom are passed over as being in the unfaithful line and extraneous to the author's purpose. Elijah is only mentioned once and Elisha is not mentioned at all. Yet just enough of the evil is recorded to show that it will be punished and to explain the captivity.

EZRA: RESTORATION

Subject The subject of Ezra is restoration.

Structure Ezra is a compilation, not a single narrative. Scroggie says that of 880 verses, 109 are narrative, 111 are registries, 44 are letters, 3 are proclamations, 3 are excerpts, and 10 are prayers. Chapters 4:8-7:18 and 8:12-26 are in Aramaic.

I.	The Return and Rebuilding of the Temple under Zerubbabel	1:1-6:22
	A. The Decree of Cyrus to Return	1:1-11
	B. The Census of the Returnees	2:1-70
	C. The Commencement of Rebuilding of the Temple	3:1-13
	D. The Cessation of Rebuilding of the Temple	4:1-24
	E. The Resumption of Rebuilding of the Temple	5:1-17
	F. The Completion of Rebuilding of the Temple	6:1-22
II.	The Return and Restoration of the People under Ezra	7:1-10:44
	A. The Decree of Artaxerxes	7:1-28
	B. The Return of Ezra	8:1-36
	C. The Confession of Ezra	9:1-15
	D. The Confrontation of the People	10:1-44

Author The author is anonymous, but it is obvious Ezra wrote the book of Ezra. Ezra 7:28-9:15 is written in the first person from Ezra's point of view. Ezra was more of a compiler than an author. The 70-year captivity is dated from 605 BC to 536 BC. Zerubbabel returned in 538 BC and was in Jerusalem in 516 BC (chs. 1-6). During Zerubbabel's time, the prophets Haggai and Zechariah ministered (around 520 BC and later). Ezra returned in 458 BC (chs. 7-10). Nehemiah came back in 445 BC. Thus, Ezra probably wrote his book between 450-440 BC. During this period, Jauutama Buddha was in India (560-450 BC), Confucius was in China (551-479 BC), and Socrates was in Greece (470-399 BC).

Recipients The recipients of Ezra were the Israelites who returned from Babylon. They also experienced the events recorded in it.

Purpose The purpose of Ezra was to show that the Lord fulfilled His promise announced by the prophets to return the people from Babylon, to rebuild the Temple, to restore the Temple worship according to the Law, and to preserve the reassembled community from relapses into idolatrous worship.

Summary: The overall message of Ezra is that God had the Temple rebuilt and the people restored.

The overall spiritual truth of Ezra is God restores to the place of worship and obedience.

Ezra 7:10 "For Ezra had prepared his heart to seek the Law of the LORD, and to do *it*, and to teach statutes and ordinances in Israel.

NEHEMIAH: CONTINUAL RESTORATION

Subject The subject of Nehemiah is repeated restoration.

Structure The key to the structure is in Nehemiah 2:12 and Nehemiah 7:5. Those verses say that God put into Nehemiah's heart to do two things: rebuild the wall and restore the population in Jerusalem. Thus, the book is divided into two parts: rebuilding the wall (chs. 1-6) and restoring the city (chs. 7-13).

I.	Rebuilding of the Wall	1:1-6:19
	A. The Prayer of Nehemiah	1:1-11
	B. The Planning of Nehemiah	2:1-20
	C. The Perspiration of the People	3:1-32
	D. The Persistence of the People	4:1-23
	E. The Prescription of Nehemiah	5:1-19
	F. The Perception of Nehemiah	6:1-19
II.	Restoration of the Community	7:1-13:31
	A. The Registry of the People	7:1-73
	B. The Reading of the Law	8:1-18
	C. The Repentance of the People	9:1-38
	D. The Ratification of the Covenant	10:1-27
	E. The Repopulation of the City	11:1-36
	F. The Rededication of the Wall	12:1-47
	G. The Restoration of the People	13:1-31

Author Nehemiah wrote the book of Nehemiah (1:1). All agree that Nehemiah 1:1-7:5, Nehemiah 12:27-43, and Nehemiah 13:4-31 are the words of Nehemiah, but beyond that, there are several theories: 1) Some think Nehemiah composed those portions and compiled the rest. 2) Others think Ezra wrote Nehemiah 7:6-12:26 and Nehemiah 12:44-13:3 and compiled the rest using Nehemiah's diaries. 3) A third view is that neither wrote it. By the way, Nehemiah 7:5-73 is almost identical to Ezra 2:1-70. Both lists may have been taken from the same document. Nehemiah served under Artaxerxes. Artaxerxes I of Persia (2:1) who reigned from 464-423 BC. Nehemiah left Persia in the 20th year of Artaxerxes (2:1), 445 BC. Nehemiah returned to Persia in the 32nd year of Artaxerxes, 432 BC (13:5). Nehemiah was in Jerusalem for 12 years. "After some time," he left Persia and returned to Jerusalem around 425 BC (13:6). Thus, Nehemiah wrote the book of Nehemiah about 425 BC.

Recipients The recipients of the book were the Israelites in Jerusalem after the captivity.

Purpose: The purpose of Nehemiah was to show that God not only restores, but He also repeatedly, constantly, and continually restores.

Summary: The overall message of Nehemiah is that God rebuilds and constantly restores.

The overall spiritual truth of Nehemiah is continual restoration.

Zerubbabel came and restored. Ezra came and restored. Now Nehemiah comes and restores twice.

Nehemiah 2:12 "Then I arose in the night, I and a few men with me; I told no one what my God had put in my heart to do at Jerusalem; nor was there any animal with me, except the one on which I rode."

Nehemiah 7:5 "Then my God put it into my heart to gather the nobles, the rulers, and the people, that they might be registered by genealogy. And I found a register of the genealogy of those who had come up in the first *return,* and found written in it."

Nehemiah 8:8 "So they read distinctly from the book, in the Law of God; and they gave the sense, and helped *them* to understand the reading."

Nehemiah 13:25 "So I contended with them and cursed them, struck some of them and pulled out their hair, and made them swear by God, *saying,* "You shall not give your daughters as wives to their sons, nor take their daughters for your sons or yourselves."

There is a sense in which Nehemiah furnishes the historical background for Malachi. He lived and ministered during Nehemiah's time. A comparison of their books reveals that many of the evils Nehemiah encountered were specifically denounced by Malachi. The cold-hearted indifference toward God, described in both books, remained a problem in Israel between the Old and New Testaments.

ESTHER: PROVIDENCE OF GOD

Subject The subject of Esther is the providence of God.
Structure Esther is almost pure narrative. It is a story.

I. The Danger to the Jews	1:1-5:14
A. The Divorce of Vashti	1:1-22
B. The Discovery of Esther	2:1-23
C. The Decree of Haman	3:1-15
D. The Decision of Esther	4:1-5:14
II. The Deliverance of the Jews	6:1-10:3
A. The Defeat of Haman	6:1-7:10
B. The Decree of Ahasuerus	8:1-17
C. The Defeat of the Enemy (Purim)	9:1-32
D. The Description of Mordecai	10:1-3

Author The author is anonymous. Mordecai was probably the author. Esther 9:20 says he was an author. Josephus held that Mordecai was the author. The author may have had access to the book of the Chronicles of the Kings of Media and Persia (2:23; 10:2). Ahasuerus was king of Persia from 486-464 BC. The feast of Ahasuerus took place in the third year, 483 BC (1:3). The historian Herodotus referred to this banquet as the occasion of Ahasuerus' planning for a military campaign against Greece. He was defeated by the Greeks at Salamis in 479 BC. Herodotus says that when the Greeks defeated Ahasuerus, he sought consolation in his harem. This corresponds to when he held a "contest" and crowned Esther Queen of Persia (2:16-17) in 478 BC. The rest of the book's events occurred in 473 BC (3:7-12). That means that the events of the book span ten years, from 483 (1:3) to 473 BC (3:7). Esther 10:2-3 probably refers to the end of Ahasuerus' reign, which was in 464 BC. The palace at Susa was destroyed by fire in about 435 BC. That is not mentioned at all in Esther. Thus, Esther was written between 464 and 435 BC.

Recipients The recipients were the Israelites living in Persia about 450 BC. Although they were disobedient by staying in Persia, they were still God's children, and He provided for them.

Purpose The purpose of Esther is to remind the Jews who remained in Persia of God's providential care.

Summary: The overall message of Esther is God providentially delivered the Jews from extinction.

The overall spiritual truth of Esther is that God providentially protects His children.

Esther 4:13-14 Mordecai said to Esther, "Do not think in your heart that you will escape in the king's palace any more than all the other Jews. For if you remain completely silent at this time, relief and deliverance will arise for the Jews from another place, but you and your father's house will perish. Yet who knows whether you have come to the kingdom for *such* a time as this?"

Some have rejected Esther because: 1) It does not mention the name of God, faith, prayer, or godly virtues. 2) It is not necessary for the line of the Messiah. 3) Neither Jesus nor the New Testament quotes it. Nevertheless, Esther should be in the Bible because 1) It is not only in the Jewish canon; it has been venerated, second only to the book of Moses and has been used regularly in the observance of the Feast of Purim. 2) Jesus accepted it (Lk. 24:44). 3) The early church accepted it.

God's name does not appear in the book, but that is the point. He works providentially. Providence says that God works "behind the scenes." He hides Himself from view, but He works things out to care for His own. Either luck is at work, or the Lord is at work. God's name is not seen, but His hand is. By the way, God's name does not occur in the Song of Solomon either (Deut. 31:18).

Esther also records the origin of the Feast of Purim, which Mordecai instituted at Esther's suggestion in memory of the deliverance of the Jews from the murderous plot of Haman. "Purim" means "lots." The name was given to the feast because of the casing of lots by Haman to decide when he should carry out the decree issued by the king for the extermination of the Jews. It was probably given in irony.

JOB: THE SUFFERING OF THE RIGHTEOUS

Subject The subject of Job is the suffering of the righteous.

Structure Job is a story, but it is not just a narrative; it is a story with a great deal of dialogue. It is more like a drama than a narrative. The key to the structure is the type of literature: Job 1:1-2:10 is prose. Job 2:11-42:6 is poetry, and Job 42:8-17 is again prose.

1. Prologue: A Righteous Man Severely Suffered — 1:1-2:10
   - A. Job's Piety and Prosperity — 1:1-5
   - B. Satan's Proposal — 1:6-12
   - C. Job's Adversity: Loss of Children and Wealth — 1:13-22
   - D. Satan's Persistence — 2:1-6
   - E. Job's Affliction: Loss of Well-being and Wife's Sympathy — 2:7-10
2. Dialogue: Why Do People Suffer? — 2:11-42:6
   - A. With Friends--first cycle — 3:1-14:22
   - B. With Friends--second cycle — 15:1-21:34
   - C. With Friends--third cycle — 21:1-31:40
   - D. With Elihu — 32:1-37:24
   - E. With God — 38:1-42:6
3. Epilogue: Sufferers Who Trust God Become More God-like — 42:7-17

Author The author is anonymous. Job probably wrote the book. The land of Uz (1:1) is adjacent to Midian, where Moses lived for forty years. Moses could have obtained the record left by Job. That would explain how the Israelites possessed this non-Israelite story and gave it canonical status. Job lived 140 years after the events of this book (42:16). His total life span must have been close to 200 years. This fits the patriarchal period (Abraham lived 175 years; Gen. 25:7). Like Abraham, Isaac, and Jacob, Job was the priest of his family and offered sacrifices, which was not allowed after the Exodus. Job uses the characteristic patriarchal name for God, Shaddai, the Almighty, thirty-one times. This early term for God is only found seventeen times in the rest of the Old Testament. The Chaldeans, who murdered Job's servants (1:17), were nomads and had not yet become city dwellers. Therefore, Job lived during the patriarchal period. If Job wrote it, it was probably written shortly after the events occurred, about 2000-1800 BC.

Recipients The recipients were the people who lived during the period of the patriarchs. The content of the book, however, addresses a universal problem of all humanity in all ages.

Purpose The purpose of Job is to teach that if the righteous trust God amid their suffering, they will grow in maturity.

Summary: The overall message of Job is that a sovereign, wise God allows the righteous to suffer, not to punish them but to purify and perfect them.

The overall truth of Job is God allows believers to suffer to purify and perfect them.

Job 1:21 "And he said: 'Naked I came from my mother's womb, and naked shall I return there. The LORD gave, and the LORD has taken away; Blessed be the name of the LORD.'"

Job 13:15 "Though He slay me, yet will I trust Him. Even so, I will defend my own ways before Him."

Job 5:7 "Yet man is born to trouble, as the sparks fly upward."

Job 14:1 "Man who is born of woman Is of few days and full of trouble.

Job 38:4 "Where were you when I laid the foundations of the earth? Tell Me, if you have understanding."

Job 42:5-6 "I have heard of You by the hearing of the ear, But now my eye sees You. Job Therefore I abhor myself, And repent in dust and ashes."

PSALMS: PRAISE

Subject The subject of Psalms is praise.

Structure If "structure" means the development of a subject or even the divisions of a subject, there is no structure to the Psalter. A better word here is "arrangement." The Midrash divides the Psalter into five parts and compares it to the five-fold division of the Torah. These divisions are marked by doxologies: 41:13, 72:18-19, 89:52, 106:48. The fifth book concludes with a series of doxologies, namely Psalms 146-150. The reason for the separate collections is unknown.

I. Book One   1:1-41:13
II. Book Two   42:1-72:20
III. Book Three   73:1-89:52
IV. Book Four   90:1-106:48
V. Book Five   107:1-150:6

Authors The Psalms were written by several men. The superscriptions are not inspired but are very old and probably accurate. According to the superscriptions, 1) David has seventy-three psalms assigned to him (3-9; 11-32; 34-41; 51-65; 68-70; 86; 101; 103; 108-110; 122; 124; 131; 133; 138-145; the New Testament assigns two others: 2; 95; see Acts 4:25; Heb. 4:7. 2). Asaph wrote twelve (50; 73-83). He was a Levite who headed the service of music (Ez. 2:41; see also 1 Chron. 16:4, 5, 7, 37). 3) The sons of Korah composed ten (42; 44-49; 84-85; 87; see 1 Chron. 9:19). 4) Solomon contributed two (72; 127). 5) Heman constructed one (88; see 1 Chron. 25:1, 5-6). 6) Ethan penned one (89; see 1 Kings 4:31.). 7) Moses authored one (90). The inscriptions leave fifty psalms anonymous (1-2; 10; 33; 43; 66-67; 71; 91-100; 102; 104-107; 111-121; 123; 125; 126; 128-130; 132; 134-137; 146-150). The New Testament identifies David as the author of two of these (2, 95). Thus, forty-eight are anonymous. The rabbis called those without a known author "orphan psalms." Moses probably wrote Psalm 90 between 1447 and 1407 BC. About half of the psalms were written by David around 1000 BC. Psalm 137 was written during the Babylonian captivity in about 580 BC. So the book was written between 1407 and 580 BC.

Recipients The psalms themselves say they were written to 1) the Lord (4:1; 5:1), 2) Israel (78:1), 3) the righteous (33:1), and 4) all mankind (150:6).

Purposes The twofold purpose of the Psalms is to inspire praise and provide prophecy. Psalms is the inspired songbook of prayer and praise. Amid their doubts and fears, longings and hopes, joys and sorrows, believers should trust God (to bless the righteous and punish the wicked) and praise God. According to the New Testament, at least thirteen psalms are Messianic (2; 8; 16; 22; 31; 40; 41; 45; 68; 69; 102; 110; 118). Over one-fourth of the Old Testament quotations in the New Testament are from the Psalms. However uncertain the times, the Lord will establish His kingdom through the future Messiah. That reassurance might not stabilize the time, but it will certainly stabilize the heart.

Summary: The overall message of the Psalms is regardless of the circumstances, trust God, praise God, and expect Messiah in the future.

The overall truth of the Psalms is the godly may lament, but the Lord is worthy of trust and praise in all circumstances.

Psalm 1:1-2 "Blessed *is* the man Who walks not in the counsel of the ungodly, Nor stands in the path of sinners, Nor sits in the seat of the scornful; but his delight *is* in the law of the LORD, And in His law he meditates day and night."

Psalm 13:1, 5 "How long, O LORD? Will You forget me forever? How long will You hide Your face from me? … But I have trusted in Your mercy; My heart shall rejoice in Your salvation."

Psalm 16:10 "For You will not leave my soul in Sheol, Nor will You allow Your Holy One to see corruption."

Psalm 23:1-6 "The LORD *is* my shepherd; I shall not want. He makes me to lie down in green pastures; He leads me beside the still waters. He restores my soul; He leads me in the paths of righteousness For His name's sake. Yea, though I walk through the valley of the shadow of death, I will fear no evil; For You *are* with me; Your rod and Your staff, they comfort me. You prepare a table before me in the presence of my enemies; You anoint my head with oil; My cup runs over. Surely goodness and mercy shall follow me All the days of my life; And I will dwell in the house of the LORD Forever."

Psalm 32:1-1-2 "Blessed *is he whose* transgression *is* forgiven, *whose* sin *is* covered. Blessed *is* the man to whom the LORD does not impute iniquity, and in whose spirit *there is* no deceit."

Psalm 42:5 "Why are you cast down, O my soul? And *why* are you disquieted within me? Hope in God, for I shall yet praise Him *For* the help of His countenance."

Psalm 51:5 "Behold, I was brought forth in iniquity, and in sin my mother conceived me."

Psalm 51:7, 13 "Purge me with hyssop, and I shall be clean; Wash me, and I shall be whiter than snow…. *Then* I will teach transgressors Your ways, And sinners shall be converted to You."

Psalm 73:3, 16-17 "For I *was* envious of the boastful, When I saw the prosperity of the wicked…. When I thought *how* to understand this, It *was* too painful for me—Until I went into the sanctuary of God; *Then* I understood their end.

Psalm 91:1-2 "He who dwells in the secret place of the Most High Shall abide under the shadow of the Almighty. I will say of the LORD, "*He is* my refuge and my fortress; My God, in Him I will trust."

Psalm 110:1 "The LORD said to my Lord, 'Sit at My right hand, Till I make Your enemies Your footstool.'"

Psalm 117:1 "Praise the LORD, all you Gentiles! Laud Him, all you peoples! For His merciful kindness is great toward us, And the truth of the LORD *endures* forever. Praise the LORD!"

Psalm 119:9 "How can a young man cleanse his way? By taking heed according to Your word."

Psalm 119:18 "Open my eyes, that I may see Wondrous things from Your law."

Psalm 124:2-3 "If it had not been the LORD who was on our side, When men rose up against us, ihen they would have swallowed us alive, When their wrath was kindled against us."

Psalm 127:1 "Unless the LORD builds the house, they labor in vain who build it; Unless the LORD guards the city, The watchman stays awake in vain."

Psalm 131:1 "LORD, my heart is not haughty, Nor my eyes lofty. neither do I concern myself with great matters, nor with things too profound for me."

Psalm 133:1 "Behold, how good and how pleasant *it is* for brethren to dwell together in unity!"

PROVERBS: WISDOM

Subject The subject of Proverbs is wisdom.

Structure Proverbs contain titles heading each section. The title "The Proverbs of Solomon" appears three times. The first time (1:1), it applies to the whole book and the other two occurrences (10:1; 25:1) apply to the sections within the book. The first nine chapters contain discourses on the value of wisdom. Then follow two collections of the proverbs of Solomon. Two appendices supplement each collection.

I. Introduction	1:1-7
II. A Father's Praise of Wisdom	1:8-9:8
III. The Proverbs of Solomon	10:1-22:16
IV. The Words of Wise Men	22:17-24:34
A. The Words of Wise Men	24:17-22
B. The Further Words of Wise Men	24:23-34
V. Hezekiah's Collection of the Proverbs of Solomon	25:1-29:27
VI. The Words of Wise Men	30:1-31:31
A. The Words of Agur	30:1-33
B. The Words of King Lemuel's Mother	31:1-31

Authors Proverbs has several authors: 1) Solomon (1:1), 2) Wise men (22:17; 24:23), 3) Agur (ch. 30), and Lemuel (ch. 31, at least he wrote 31:1-9). Nothing is known about these two authors except that they wrote proverbs. Solomon wrote about 950 BC. At least part of the book was addressed to his son, presumably Rehoboam (1:8; 2:1; etc.). This applies to Proverbs 1:1-9:18 for sure and probably Proverbs 10:1-22:16. It more than likely does not apply to Proverbs 25:1ff. Proverbs 25:1 says that a larger portion of the book was compiled by the men of Hezekiah. That was not until 710 BC. Isaiah and Micah ministered during Hezekiah's time. It has been suggested that they were involved in the collection of the Proverbs.

Recipients The primary recipients of most of the Proverbs were Solomon's children (1:8; 2:1; 4:1). Proverbs 8:1-5 indicates that the book was for all humanity in general. While God's Law is assumed everywhere, Israel is never mentioned. It is not a Jewish book. There is a universality to this book. These proverbs apply to all people at all times in all places.

Purposes The twofold purpose of Proverbs is to impart moral discernment (1:2a, 3-5) and develop mental clarity and perception (1:2b, 6). The philosophy of this book is not "live and learn" but "learn and live."

Summary: The overall message is that proverbs assist the wise and the unwise in developing mental acumen and wisdom (skill) for living.

The overall spiritual truth is the wise learn wisdom from God's Word and from watching wise people.

Proverbs 1:7 "The fear of the LORD is the beginning of knowledge, but fools despise wisdom and instruction."
Proverbs 9:10 "The fear of the LORD is the beginning of wisdom, and the knowledge of the Holy One is understanding."

Proverbs 3:5-6 "Trust in the LORD with all your heart, And lean not on your own understanding; In all your ways acknowledge Him, And He shall direct your paths."
Proverbs 4:23 "Keep your heart with all diligence, for out of it *spring* the issues of life."
Proverbs 12:25 "Anxiety in the heart of man causes depression, but a good word makes it glad.
Proverbs 13:24 "He who spares his rod hates his son, but he who loves him disciplines him promptly."
Proverbs 14:34 "Righteousness exalts a nation, But sin is a reproach to any people. What does the Bible say spare the rod spoil the child."
Proverbs 17:22 "A merry heart does good, *like* medicine, but a broken spirit dries the bones."

Proverbs 21:9 "Better to dwell in a corner of a housetop, Than in a house shared with a contentious woman."
Proverbs 21:19 "Better to dwell in the wilderness, Than with a contentious and angry woman."

Proverbs 23:7 "For as he thinks in his heart, so *is* he. 'Eat and drink!' he says to you, but his heart is not with you."

Proverbs 26:4 "Do not answer a fool according to his folly, lest you also be like him."
Proverbs 26:5 "Answer a fool according to his folly, lest he be wise in his own eyes."

ECCLESIASTES: THE FUTILITY OF LIFE

Subject The subject of Ecclesiastes is the futility of life.

Structure Ecclesiastes begins with a prologue (1:2-11) and ends with an epilogue (12:8-12). It starts and stops with the same statement, "vanity of vanity … all is vanity" (1:2; 12:8). Vanity does not mean "foolish pride." The Hebrew word translated "vanity" means "breath, vapor, emptiness." Transitory, frail, futile, and unsatisfying is the idea. There are four broad discourses, each ending with a conclusion: 1) Eccl. 1:12-2:26 (2:24-26), 2) Eccl. 3:1-5:20 (5:18-20), 3) Eccl. 6:1-8:17 (8:15-17), 4) Eccl. 9:1-12:7 (12:1-7). There are sections within these divisions, which also have conclusions (3:12, 22; 9:7-9; 11:7-10), but these four are the major divisions

I.	Prologue: Life is Futile	1:1-11
II.	The First Discourse: Futility of Wisdom, Pleasure, etc.	1:12-2:26
III.	The Second Discourse: Futility of Various Areas of Life	3:1-5:20
IV.	The Third Discourse: Futility of Attainments	6:1-8:17
V.	The Fourth Discourse: Futility in Uncertainties and Old Age	9:1-12:8
VI.	Epilogue: Fear God and Keep His Commands	12:9-14

Author The author is Solomon (1:1). There is an ancient Jewish tradition that Solomon wrote the Song of Solomon in his youth, Proverbs when he was middle-aged, and Ecclesiastes in the evening of his days. If that is the case, he wrote on love as a young man, wisdom as he grew old, and futility as an old man. Solomon probably wrote Ecclesiastes in 935 BC.

Recipients The book is not specifically addressed to anyone except to a "young man" mentioned in Ecclesiastes 11:9 and Solomon's reference to "my son" in Ecclesiastes 12:12.

Purpose The purpose of Ecclesiastes is to teach that even though life is futile, believers are to trust and obey God.

Summary: The overall message of Ecclesiastes is that even though life is futile, we are to fear God and enjoy life.

The overall spiritual truth is even though life is futile, it is a gift from God, which means that we should enjoy it and, at the same time, trust and obey the Lord.

The phrase "under the sun" refers to all of life. Life is futile, with or without God. The author says that throughout the book and at the end of it (3:14; 12:13-14). Life is filled with iniquities, uncertainties, changes in fortune, and violations of justice. But the book is not pessimistic. It teaches that we are to enjoy life and trust God. In other words, Solomon is saying that God has not revealed everything. There is a mystery to life. We only know what God has chosen to tell us, yet life is not a puzzle that wisdom unlocks. It is a gift given to us by God to enjoy and use responsibly.

Ecclesiastes 1:2 "'Vanity of vanities,' says the Preacher; 'Vanity of vanities, all *is* vanity.'"

Ecclesiastes 3:11 "He has made everything beautiful in its time. Also, He has put eternity in their hearts, except that no one can find out the work that God does from beginning to end."

Ecclesiastes 3:13 "And also that every man should eat and drink and enjoy the good of all his labor—it *is* the gift of God."

Ecclesiastes 8:11 "Because the sentence against an evil work is not executed speedily, therefore the heart of the sons of men is fully set in them to do evil."

Ecclesiastes 9:9-10 "Live joyfully with the wife whom you love all the days of your vain life which He has given you under the sun, all your days of vanity; for that *is* your portion in life, and in the labor which you perform under the sun. Whatever your hand finds to do, do *it* with your might; for *there is* no work or device or knowledge or wisdom in the grave where you are going. \

Ecclesiastes 9:11 "I returned and saw under the sun that—The race *is* not to the swift, nor the battle to the strong, nor bread to the wise, nor riches to men of understanding, nor favor to men of skill; but time and chance happen to them all."

Ecclesiastes 11:9-10, 12:1 "Rejoice, O young man, in your youth, And let your heart cheer you in the days of your youth; Walk in the ways of your heart, And in the sight of your eyes; But know that for all these God will bring you into judgment. Therefore remove sorrow from your heart, And put away evil from your flesh, For childhood and youth *are* vanity. Remember now your Creator in the days of your youth, Before the difficult days come, And the years draw near when you say, "I have no pleasure in them.""

Ecclesiastes 12:13-14 "Let us hear the conclusion of the whole matter: Fear God and keep His commandments, For this is man's all. For God will bring every work into judgment, Including every secret thing, Whether good or evil."

There are basically three theories concerning the author's point of view. The philosophical hypothesis says that "under the sun" means "apart from God" and that the author is a wise man who comes to faith by reason. The problem with that hypothesis is that "under the sun" does not mean apart from God (8:15). The experiential approach is that "under the sun" means life apart from God and, as a backslider, Solomon discovered that life apart from God was empty. Again, the problem is that "under the sun" does not mean apart from God (8:15). The spiritual view contends that the author is not a philosopher or a repentant backslider but a deeply spiritual man. He is simply saying that life with or without God is a mystery. As an old, wise, and godly man, he says, "When I see life, it seems to me it is empty and aimless." There are aimless cycles (1:4 ff.) and inexplicable paradoxes (4:1; 7:15; 8:8). One might conclude that all is futile since it is impossible to discern any purpose in the ordering of events. Yet life is a gift of God and is to be enjoyed. The wise people will live their lives in obedience to God, recognizing that God will eventually judge all human beings (3:16-17; 12:14).

SONG OF SOLOMON: ROMANTIC LOVE

Subject The subject of the Song of Solomon is romantic love.

Structure The form of the Song is somewhere between a loose connection of songs and a drama. It has been called a lyrical poem with a dramatic form of dialogue, a dramatic poem built on a dialogue, and a lyrical ballad, the point being that it is a unified lyrical song with a dramatic form. What, then, is its structure? It has been divided into six acts, with two scenes in each act and into only five parts. This much is clear: three times, the maid adjures the daughters of Jerusalem (2:7; 3:5; 8:4) and 5:1 may be a concluding formula.

I.	First Stanza: Courtship	1:2-2:7
II	Second Stanza: Courtship continued	2:8-3:5
III.	Third Stanza: Marriage and honeymoon	3:6-5:1
IV.	Fourth Stanza: The honeymoon is over	5:2-6:9
V.	Fifth Stanza: The marriage deepens	6:10-8:4
VI.	Sixth Stanza: The maturity of love	8:5-14

Author The author is Solomon (1:1). Solomon's name appears seven times in the book (1:1, 5; 3:7, 9, 11; 8:11-12). Five of these are connected with the actual appearances of Solomon in action (3:7, 9, 11; 8:11-12), whereas one mentions "the curtains of Solomon" as a simile (1:5). Solomon probably wrote the Song early in his reign, about 970 BC.

Recipients The recipients were the Israelites who lived during the lifetime of Solomon.

Purpose The purpose of the Song of Solomon is to exalt the joys of romantic love. It is a bold and positive endorsement by God of marital love in all its physical and emotional beauty.

Summary: The overall message of the Song of Solomon is there is joy in the romantic love between a man and a woman.

The overall spiritual truth of the Song of Solomon is husbands and wives are to enjoy marital love.

How can a man with a harem of 140 women (6:8) extol a Shulamite as though she were his only bride? The answer may be that his relationship with her was the only pure romance he ever experienced. After all, the bulk of his marriages were political arrangements.

Song of Solomon 1:2 "Let him kiss me with the kisses of his mouth—For your love *is* better than wine."

Song of Solomon 2:15 "Catch us the foxes, the little foxes that spoil the vines, For our vines *have* tender grapes."

Song of Solomon 7:10 "I *am* my beloved's, and his desire *is* toward me."

<u>**Song of Solomon 8:6-7**</u> "Set me as a seal upon your heart, as a seal upon your arm; For love *is as* strong as death, jealousy *as* cruel as the grave; Its flames *are* flames of fire, A most vehement flame. Many waters cannot quench love, nor can the floods drown it. If a man would give for love All the wealth of his house, It would be utterly despised."

There are three different interpretations of the Song of Solomon. The allegorical interpretation says fictional people and events are used as symbols to suggest a deeper or hidden meaning. The typological method differs from the allegorical method in that it maintains the story's historicity. In an allegory, the events may or may not be historical. In a type, the events are always real historical events. The literal view interprets the song as literally depicting the love of a man for a woman and stops short of seeing a deeper meaning. As has been said, "When the plain sense of Scripture makes common sense, seek no further sense." The literal interpretation, however, does not mean that the book has no spiritual illustrations and applications. It illustrates God's love for His covenant people, Israel, and anticipates Christ's love for His bride, the church (Eph. 5:31-32), but this is an application, not the primary interpretation.

ISAIAH: THE SALVATION OF GOD

Subject The subject of Isaiah is the salvation of God.

Structure Most of Isaiah is poetry. Chapters 1-35 are in the form of poems, followed by four chapters of history. Chapters 40-66 are, again, poetry.

I.	Prophecies of Judgment and Restoration (Salvation)	1:1-35:10
	A. Judgment on Judah	1:1-12:6.
	B. Judgment on the Nations	13:1-23:18
	C. The Future Tribulation and Kingdom	24:1-27:13
	D. Six Woes	28:1-33
	E. The Future Tribulation and Kingdom	34:1-35:10
II.	History under Hezekiah	36:1-39:8
	A. Hezekiah's Distress and Deliverance	36:1-37:38
	B. Hezekiah's Sickness and Sin	38:1-39:8
III.	Prophecies of Restoration (Salvation)	40:1-66:24
	A. The Comfort of God	40:1-48:22
	B. The Servant of God	49:1-57:21
	C. The Kingdom of God	58:1-66:24

Author Isaiah is the author (1:1). John 12:37-41 quotes Isaiah 6:9-10 and Isaiah 53:1, attributing them to Isaiah. Paul quotes Isaiah (in Rom. 9:27, he quotes Israel 10:22-23 and Isaiah 1:9; in Rom. 10:16-21, he quotes Isaiah 53:1 and Isaiah 65:2) and gives the credit to Isaiah. The same is true of Matthew 3:3, 12:17, Luke 3:4-6, and Acts 8:28. Furthermore, Jewish and Christian traditions have universally attributed the book to Isaiah. Isaiah wrote about 680 BC.

Recipients The recipients were Israelites who lived in the Southern Kingdom about 680 BC. Hosea and Micah were his contemporaries. When Isaiah was young, Assyria was a menacing power. Nations wanted to form a coalition against her. King Ahaz would not join them, so Syria and the Northern Kingdom attacked the Southern Kingdom to force her to cooperate with them. Instead of trusting the Lord for help, Ahaz turned to Assyria for assistance! Assyria defeated the Northern Kingdom in 722 BC and the Southern Kingdom became a vassal state. Then, Assyria attacked Judah. Isaiah told the people to trust the Lord, but others told the king to turn to Egypt for help. God gave Hezekiah the victory by miraculously defeating Sennacherib (chs. 37-38). Isaiah warned Judah of judgment by Babylon, even though Babylon had not yet risen to power. He delivered a warning to the Northern Kingdom (28:1), pronounced judgment on Gentile nations (Babylon, Moab, Damascus, Egypt, etc.), and spoke to all the people of the earth.

Purpose The purpose of Isaiah is to preach against (expose) sin, pronounce judgment, and predict the salvation of God. Isaiah predicted that Assyria would not take the Southern Kingdom (chs. 36-39). He also predicted the Kingdom of God and the Messiah.

Summary: The overall message of Isaiah is sin will be judged, but salvation is coming through the Messiah and the kingdom.

The overall spiritual truth of Isaiah is that God judges sin and brings salvation through the Messiah and the kingdom.

Isaiah 1:18 "'Come now, and let us reason together,' Says the LORD, 'Though your sins are like scarlet, They shall be as white as snow; Though they are red like crimson, They shall be as wool.'"

Isaiah 6:1, 5 "In the year that King Uzziah died, I saw the Lord sitting on a throne, high and lifted up, and the train of His robe filled the temple. So I said: 'Woe is me, for I am undone! Because I am a man of unclean lips, And I dwell in the midst of a people of unclean lips; For my eyes have seen the King, The LORD of hosts.'"

Isaiah 7:14 "Therefore the Lord Himself will give you a sign: Behold, the virgin shall conceive and bear a Son, and shall call His name Immanuel."

Isaiah 9:6-7 "For unto us a Child is born, unto us a Son is given; and the government will be upon His shoulder. And His name will be called Wonderful, Counselor, Mighty God, Everlasting Father, Prince of Peace. Of the increase of His government and peace There will be no end, Upon the throne of David and over His kingdom, To order it and establish it with judgment and justice From that time forward, even forever. The zeal of the Lord of hosts will perform this"

Isaiah 11:1-2 "There shall come forth a Rod from the stem of Jesse, And a Branch shall grow out of his roots. The Spirit of the LORD shall rest upon Him, The Spirit of wisdom and understanding, The Spirit of counsel and might, The Spirit of knowledge and of the fear of the LORD.

Isaiah 26:3 "You will keep him in perfect peace, Whose mind is stayed on You, Because he trusts in You."

Isaiah 40:31 "But those who wait on the LORD Shall renew their strength; They shall mount up with wings like eagles, They shall run and not be weary, They shall walk and not faint."

Isaiah 53:5-6 "But He was wounded for our transgressions, He was bruised for our iniquities; The chastisement for our peace was upon Him, And by His stripes, we are healed. All we like sheep have gone astray; We have turned, everyone, to his own way; And the LORD has laid on Him the iniquity of us all."

JEREMIAH: THE JUDGMENT OF GOD

Subject The subject of Jeremiah is the judgment of God.

Structure Jeremiah is a combination of history, biography, and prophecy. The closest thing to a literary structure is a series of messages. In chapters 2-20, each message begins with "the word of the Lord came." In chapters 21-39, the same phrase is used and a historical reference is added. So, the structure of Jeremiah is topical, not chronological (not even necessarily logical).

I.	Introduction: The Call and Commission of Jeremiah	1
II.	Judgment against Judah and Jerusalem	2-45
	A. Messages Indicting the People	2-20
	B. Messages Announcing the Captivity	21-39
	C. Messages to the Remnant after the Captivity	40-45
III.	Judgment against the Nations	46-51
IV.	Appendix	52

Author Jeremiah was the author (1:1). Jeremiah dictated all of his prophecies to Baruch (36:1-4). That scroll was destroyed (36:23). Jeremiah dictated another edition (36:22). That edition is not the present book. Jeremiah wrote the book in our Bible, but many sections show evidence of being composed in the latter part of his ministry. Chapter 52 is almost identical to 2 Kings 24:18-25:30 and was probably added by Baruch. Jeremiah's ministry stretched from 627 BC to *ca.* 580 BC. Jeremiah was weitten *ca.* 580 BC or shortly after that.

Recipients The recipients were the Israelites in Babylon. In 701 BC, Sennacherib attacked Jerusalem, which was miraculously spared (36-37). After that, it slipped away from the Lord. Wicked kings even introduced idolatry. Jeremiah was called to be a prophet in the thirteenth year of the reign of Josiah (1:1; 627 BC, about sixty years after the death of Isaiah). In 622 BC, the Law of Moses was rediscovered and Josiah, Israel's last good king, instituted spiritual reforms. Unfortunately, his efforts were not enough to stem the tide. After his death, the wickedness grew worse and worse. As the apostasy worsened, opposition to Jeremiah mounted. Jehoiachim destroyed his writings. In 605 BC, Nebuchadnezzar took Palestine and deported key people such as Daniel to Babylon. Jehoiachim was not a Babylonian vassal, but he rejected Jeremiah's warnings and, in 601 BC, rebelled against Babylon. There was another invasion in 597 BC. Nebuchadnezzar overthrew Jerusalem in 586 BC. Jeremiah ended up in Egypt (Ch. 52) and maybe Babylon (tradition). Jeremiah's ministry, then, stretched from 627 to *ca.* 580 BC. The main body of the book is addressed to Judah and Jerusalem (2:2; 4:2; 6:1; 7:1; etc.). In chapters 46-51, he prophesies against ten nations. He was a contemporary of Zephaniah, Habakkuk, Daniel, and Ezekiel.

Purpose The purpose of Jeremiah is to remind Israel that God judges His people in the world, but He will bring His program to pass.

Summary: The overall message of Jeremiah is Judah and the world will be judged, but there is hope in the near and distant future.

The overall spiritual message of Jeremiah is that even though God judges His people and the world, He will send the Messiah and establish His kingdom.

Jeremiah 1:5 "Before I formed you in the womb I knew you; Before you were born, I sanctified you; I ordained you a prophet to the nations."

Jeremiah 1:8 "Do not be afraid of their faces, For I *am* with you to deliver you," says the LORD."

Jeremiah 9:24 "But let him who glories glory in this, That he understands and knows Me, That I *am* the LORD, exercising lovingkindness, judgment, and righteousness in the earth. For in these I delight," says the LORD."

Jeremiah 29:11-13 "For I know the thoughts that I think toward you, says the LORD, thoughts of peace and not of evil, to give you a future and a hope. Then you will call upon Me and go and pray to Me, and I will listen to you. And you will seek Me and find *Me,* when you search for Me with all your heart."

Jeremiah 31:31-34 "Behold, the days are coming, says the LORD, when I will make a new covenant with the house of Israel and with the house of Judah—not according to the covenant that I made with their fathers in the day *that* I took them by the hand to lead them out of the land of Egypt, My covenant which they broke, though I was a husband to them, says the LORD. But this *is* the covenant that I will make with the house of Israel after those days, says the LORD: I will put My law in their minds, and write it on their hearts; and I will be their God, and they shall be My people. No more shall every man teach his neighbor, and every man his brother, saying, 'Know the LORD,' for they all shall know Me, from the least of them to the greatest of them, says the LORD. For I will forgive their iniquity, and their sin, I will remember no more."

Jeremiah 33:3 "Call to Me, and I will answer you, and show you great and mighty things, which you do not know."

In almost every chapter from 21-39 (except those dealing with the restoration of Israel, namely Jer. 30, 31, 33 and three others, Jer. 23, 26, and 36), the coming of Nebuchadnezzar is mentioned. The one coming to judge is intimated earlier (Jer. 2:37; 4:6; 7, 12, 13; 5:6; 6:1-7, 22; 8:16; 13:21; 20:4), but he is not distinctly mentioned by name until Jeremiah 21:2.

LAMENTATIONS: THE LAMENT

Subject The subject of Lamentations is a lament over the destruction of Jerusalem.

Structure Lamentations consists of five poems, one per chapter. Each poem is an acrostic, that is, each verse begins with a word whose first letter is successively one of the twenty-two letters of the Hebrew alphabet, except in chapter 3, where three verses are allotted to each letter. Four chapters were also written in what is called "limping meter," a cadence used in funeral dirges and, thus, appropriate for this lament over the destruction of Jerusalem. While there is deep emotion on the part of the writer, what he writes is the product of reflection and deliberation.

I.	The First Lament: The Desolation of Jerusalem	1:1-22
II.	The Second Lament: The Destruction of Jerusalem	2:1-22
III.	The Third Lament: Distress of Jeremiah	3:1-66
IV.	The Fourth Lament: Defeat of Jerusalem	4:1-22
V.	The Fifth Lament: Desire of Jeremiah	5:1-22

Author Lamentations is anonymous, yet there is little doubt that the author was Jeremiah. Consider the following: 1) The book is a lament. Jeremiah wrote a lament for Josiah (2 Chron. 35:25). 2) The book was written by an eyewitness of Jerusalem's siege, fall, and destruction (1:13-15; 2:6, 9; 4:1-12). Jeremiah witnessed Jerusalem's fall and remained behind after the captives were deported (Ch. 39). 3) Elements of style are similar to Jeremiah. The similarities are striking and numerous, especially in the poetic sections of Jeremiah (*cf.* Lam. 1:2 with Jer. 40:13; Lam. 1:15 with Jer. 8:21; Lam. 1:16, 2:11 with Jer. 9:1, 18; Lam. 2:22 with Jer. 6:25; and Lam. 4:21 with Jer. 49:12). The word "daughter" occurs about twenty times in each book. The same grief over Judah's downfall is evident in both books. 4) A strong and persistent tradition from the third century BC maintains that Jeremiah wrote the book. Nebuchadnezzar's siege on Jerusalem was from January 588 BC to July 586 BC. Jerusalem fell on July 18, 586 BC and on August 15, 586 BC, the city and the Temple were burned. Jeremiah probably wrote not long after the destruction before he was taken into Egypt (Jer. 43:1-7). So, the date is late 586 BC.

Recipients The recipients were the Israelites, who observed the destruction of Jerusalem (1:12), the Lord (1:20; 2:20; etc.), Judah and Jerusalem (2:13; 3:40, 41, etc.), as well as Edom (4:21-22).

Purpose The purposes of Lamentations are to express mourning over Jerusalem's holocaust, confess sins and acknowledge God's righteous judgment, and express hope in God's future restoration of His people. God has judged but will be faithful to His covenant promise (3:22-23).

Summary: The overall message of Lamentations is to lament the destruction of Jerusalem and recognize that God is righteous in judging and will be faithful to His people.

The overall spiritual truth is sin brings lamentation, but God is faithful to His promise to be merciful.

Lamentations 3:22 "*Through* the LORD's mercies we are not consumed, Because His compassions fail not."
Lamentations 3:23 "*They are* new every morning; Great *is* Your faithfulness.
Lamentations 3:24 "The LORD *is* my portion," says my soul, "Therefore I hope in Him!"
Lamentations 3:25 "The LORD *is* good to those who wait for Him, To the soul *who* seeks Him."
Lamentations 3:26 "*It is* good that *one* should hope and wait quietly For the salvation of the LORD."

EZEKIEL: THE GLORY OF GOD

Subject The subject of Ezekiel is the glory of God.

Structure Ezekiel is a series of messages (6:1; 7:1; 12:1; 13:1; 15:1; etc.). These include visions, parables, an allegory, and a direct address, all used to give a message. Any "structure" is a topical arrangement of that material. Ezekiel sees the glory of God when he is called and commissioned (1:28; 3:12, 23). He records the departure of God's glory (9:3; 10:4; 18-19; 11:22-23) and the restoration of God's glory during the millennium (43:1-5; 44:4).

I.   Introduction: Ezekiel's Call and Commission: Glory Revealed   1:1-3:27
II. Prophecies against Judah and Jerusalem: Glory Removed   4:1-24:27
III. Prophecies against the Surrounding Nations   25:1-32:32
IV. Prophecies of Israel's Restoration: Glory Restored   33:1-48:35

Author The author of Ezekiel was Ezekiel (1:3; 24:24). This autobiographical book uses the first person singular throughout. Ezekiel was born about 622 BC (1:1). In 605 BC, Nebuchadnezzar conquered Jerusalem and carried off hostages, including Daniel. Ezekiel was sixteen years old at the time. Nebuchadnezzar returned in 597 BC and carried off 10,000 captives, including Ezekiel. In other words, when Ezekiel was about twenty-five years old, he was deported to Babylon. At approximately thirty, he received his prophetic commission (1:2-3) in about 593 BC. In 586 BC, Nebuchadnezzar made his final siege of Jerusalem. Ezekiel continued his ministry until at least 570 BC and probably died about 560 BC. He, no doubt, wrote the book shortly after the incidents recorded in it. His ministry lasted at least twenty-two years (1:2; 29:17). So his book was probably completed by 565 BC.

Recipients The recipients of Ezekiel were the Israelites in captivity in Babylon about 565 BC. He addresses the book to the children of Israel (2:3, 3:1), especially those in captivity (3:11; 11:25). There are also messages for the Gentiles (25:3; 27:3; etc.). The discouraged exiles complained that "the way of the Lord is not equal" (right or just; 18:25, 29; 33:17, 20). False prophets in Babylon led some of the first captives to believe that Jerusalem would not be destroyed, that their beloved city would be spared, and they would soon return. Jeremiah heard that and wrote them a letter (ch. 29). Ezekiel began his ministry the following year, endorsing all Jeremiah said. He had to convince them that they had to return to the Lord before they could return to the land.

Purpose The purpose of Ezekiel is to show that God was justified in withdrawing His glory and to assure them that God's glory would return.

Summary: The overall message of Ezekiel is to inform the captives in Babylon that God was just withdrawing His glory from Israel, but He would also judge the Gentiles and restore His glory to Israel.

The overall spiritual truth of Ezekiel is that sin results in the departure of God's glory, but as promised, God's glory will return when Christ returns.

Ezekiel 18:20 "The soul who sins shall die. The son shall not bear the guilt of the father, nor the father bear the guilt of the son. The righteousness of the righteous shall be upon himself, and the wickedness of the wicked shall be upon himself.

Ezekiel 36:24-28 "For I will take you from among the nations, gather you out of all countries, and bring you into your own land. Then I will sprinkle clean water on you, and you shall be clean; I will cleanse you from all your filthiness and from all your idols. I will give you a new heart and put a new spirit within you; I will take the heart of stone out of your flesh and give you a heart of flesh. I will put My Spirit within you and cause you to walk in My statutes, and you will keep My judgments and do them. Then you shall dwell in the land that I gave to your fathers; you shall be My people, and I will be your God."

DANIEL: THE SOVEREIGNTY OF GOD

Subject The subject of Daniel is the sovereignty of God.

Structure Daniel is not in chronological order. Daniel 7:1 is the first year of Belshazzar, whereas Daniel 5:1 records his death. The book is written in two languages. Daniel 1:1-2:3 and Daniel 8:1-12:13 are in Hebrew, while Daniel 2:4-7:18 is in Aramaic.

I. Introduction	1:1-2:3
II. The Sovereign God will Ultimately Judge Gentile Nations	2:4-7:28
A. The Great Image	2:4-49
B. The Gold Statue	3:1-30
C. The Gigantic Tree	4:1-37
D. The Gala Feast	5:1-31
E. The Ghastly Plot	6:1-28
F. The Grotesque Beast	7:1-28
III. The Sovereign God will Ultimately Resurrect and Reward Israel	8:1-12
A. The Vision of the Ram and Goat	8:1-27
B. The Vision of Seventy Weeks	9:1-27
C. The Vision of Israel's Future	10:1-12:13

Author The author is Daniel (12:4). He uses the first person singular from Daniel 7:2 to the end. The Jewish Talmud agrees. Christ attributes it to him (Mt. 24:15; Dan. 9:27). In the third year of King Jehoiachim (605 BC), Daniel was taken, along with others, to Babylon (1:1-2). He was a teenager at the time. He ministered during the Babylonian captivity and after Babylon was overcome by the Medes and the Persians (539 BC). He was in the courts of Babylon (Nebuchadnezzar and Belshazzar) and Persia (Darius and Cyrus). He ministered at least until the third year of Cyrus (10:15; 536 BC). He probably wrote ca. 530 BC in his nineteenth year.

Recipients The recipients were the Israelites in Babylon. A Gentile nation had conquered Jerusalem. The Jews in captivity wanted to know what would happen to Israel and what would happen to the Gentile nations.

Purpose: The purpose of Daniel is to demonstrate that a sovereign God will judge the Gentile nations and restore and reward Israel. He will establish His Messianic Kingdom, which will last forever.

Summary: The overall message of Daniel is that a sovereign God will ultimately judge the Gentile nations, restore and reward Israel, and establish His kingdom.

The overall spiritual truth is that God has been sovereign over all the world's nations throughout its history.

Daniel 2:21 "And He changes the times and the seasons; He removes kings and raises up kings; He gives wisdom to the wise And knowledge to those who have understanding."

Daniel 3:17-18 "If that is the case, our God whom we serve is able to deliver us from the burning fiery furnace, and He will deliver us from your hand, O king. But if not, let it be known to you, O king, that we do not serve your gods, nor will we worship the gold image which you have set up."

Daniel 4:17 "This decision *is* by the decree of the watchers, And the sentence by the word of the holy ones, In order that the living may know that the Most High rules in the kingdom of men, Gives it to whomever He will, and sets over it the lowest of men."

Daniel 9:24-27 "Seventy weeks are determined for your people and for your holy city, To finish the transgression, To make an end of sins, To make reconciliation for iniquity, To bring in everlasting righteousness, To seal up vision and prophecy, And to anoint the Most Holy. Know therefore and understand, that from the going forth of the command To restore and build Jerusalem Until Messiah the Prince, there shall be seven weeks and sixty-two weeks; The street shall be built again, and the wall, Even in troublesome times. And after the sixty-two weeks Messiah shall be cut off, but not for Himself; And the people of the prince who is to come Shall destroy the city and the sanctuary. The end of it shall be with a flood, And till the end of the war desolations are determined. Then he shall confirm a covenant with many for one week; But in the middle of the week He shall bring an end to sacrifice and offering. And on the wing of abominations shall be one who makes desolate, even until the consummation, which is determined, Is poured out on the desolate."

Daniel 12:1-4 "At that time Michael shall stand up, The great prince who stands watch over the sons of your people; and there shall be a time of trouble, Such as never was since there was a nation, Even to that time. And at that time, your people shall be delivered, everyone who is found written in the book. And many of those who sleep in the dust of the earth shall awake, Some to everlasting life, Some to shame and everlasting contempt. Those who are wise shall shine Like the brightness of the firmament, and those who turn many to righteousness Like the stars forever and ever. but you, Daniel, shut up the words and seal the book until the time of the end; many shall run to and fro and knowledge shall increase."

HOSEA: THE LOVE OF GOD

Subject The subject of Hosea is the love of God (2:1, 2:23, and especially 14:4).

Structure The overall structure is Hosea's marriage (chs. 1-3) and Hosea's message (chs. 4-14). The details are much more difficult. The main subject in those first three chapters is Hosea's marriage, but the text repeatedly lapses into a discussion of Israel. Chapters 4-14 are even more difficult. There seems to be no order. Keil, however, suggests a three-fold division of chapters 4-14. Three promises make the three divisions (4:1-6:3; 6:4-11:11; 11:12-14:9).

I.	The Marriage of Hosea: His Love for an Unfaithful Wife	1-3
	A. Hosea's Marriage	1:2-2:1
	B. Hosea's Divorce	2:3-2:23
	C. Hosea's Remarriage	3:1-5
II.	The Message of Hosea: God's Love for Unfaithful People	4-14
	A. Round One (Indictment)	4:1-6:3
	B. Round Two (Judgment)	6:4-11:11
	C. Round Three: (Restoration)	11:12-14:9

Author Hosea wrote the book (1:1). He ministered in the Northern Kingdom (5:1). Hosea began his ministry in the reign of Jeroboam II in the north and Uzziah in the south, ca. 755 BC. He prophesied until Hezekiah, who did not start his reign until 715 BC, but his book does not mention the destruction of the Northern Kingdom in 722 BC. So, even though he ministered longer, the date of the book is probably about 725 BC. His contemporaries were Amos in the North and Isaiah and Micah in the South.

Recipients The recipients were the Israelites living in the Northern Kingdom about 725 BC. When Hosea began his ministry, Israel enjoyed peace, plenty, prosperity, and perversity (idolatry). When Jeroboam II died, his strong hand, which had curbed lawlessness, was removed and Israel began to crumble. Anarchy and assassination followed. Laxity and looseness characterized personal behavior. Courts were corrupt; judges made their living from bribes. Robbery, murder, and organized vice were visible everywhere. Even the priests were corrupt. They were at the head of organized bandit gangs! They led people into sin, making sinning attractive. Worship was formal and professional.

Purpose The purpose of Hosea is to exhibit God's case against spiritually adulterous Israel and to express God's love for Israel. God loved Israel like the husband of an unfaithful, adulterous woman who would go and reclaim his wife from the slave market (2 Tim. 2:11-13).

Summary: The overall message is even though Israel has been unfaithful to God, He will eventually restore her.

The overall spiritual truth is even when we are unfaithful, God loves us and wants to restore us to fellowship with Himself.

Hosea 4:1 "Hear the word of the LORD, You children of Israel, For the LORD *brings* a charge against the inhabitants of the land: "There is no truth or mercy Or knowledge of God in the land."

Hosea 4:6 "My people are destroyed for lack of knowledge. Because you have rejected knowledge, I also will reject you from being priest for Me; Because you have forgotten the law of your God, I also will forget your children."

Hosea 6:6 "For I desire mercy and not sacrifice, And the knowledge of God more than burnt offerings."

Hosea 11:1 "When Israel *was* a child, I loved him, And out of Egypt I called My son."

Hosea 13:4 "Yet I *am* the LORD your God ever since the land of Egypt, and you shall know no God but Me; For *there is* no savior besides Me."

Hosea 14:2 "Take words with you, And return to the LORD. Say to Him, "Take away all iniquity; Receive *us* graciously, For we will offer the sacrifices of our lips."

JOEL: THE DAY OF THE LORD

Subject The subject of Joel is the Day of the Lord (1:15; 2:11, 2:31; 3:14).

Structure Joel begins with a current local locust infestation and uses that to talk about the future situation.

Introduction	1:1
II. The Day of the Lord Foreshadowed	1:2-20
A. The Destruction of the Locusts	1:2-14
B. The Destruction of a Drought	1:15-20
III. The Day of the Lord Foretold	2:1-3:21
A. The Judgment of God	2:1-11
B. The Invitation to Israel	2:12-17
C. The Coming of the Holy Spirit	2:18-27
D. The Judgment on Gentiles	3:1-16
E. The Blessing on Israel	3:17-21

Author Joel was the author of the book (1:1). There is also evidence of borrowing between Joel and Amos (*cf.* Joel 3:16 with Amos 1:2 and Joel 3:18 with Hosea 9:13). The context suggests Hosea, an eighth-century prophet, borrowed from Joel. Many scholars have concluded that overall, the most likely time of Joel was during the reign of Joash (835-796 BC). Since there is no mention of idolatry, it may have been written after the purge of Baal worship and most other forms of idolatry in the early reign of Joash (830 BC). Joel was a contemporary of Elisha.

Recipients Joel addresses to all the inhabitants of the land (1:2). Evidently, that refers to the land of Judah, which can be seen from various references in the book, such as Joel 3:1, 3:17, etc. (in Joel 3:2, Israel is a prophetic reference to all twelve tribes).

Purpose The purpose of Joel is to call Judah to repentance and to announce the future Day of the Lord in which the Lord will judge the nations, deliver Israel, and take up His dwelling in their midst. The unprecedented locust plague was only a foretaste of the future day of the Lord.

Summary: The overall message of Joel is to announce the future Day of the Lord and call Judah to repentance.

The overall spiritual truth is that since God judges now and will judge in the future, He calls people to repentance.

Joel 2:13 "So rend your heart, and not your garments; return to the LORD your God, for He *is* gracious and merciful, slow to anger, and of great kindness; and He relents from doing harm."

Joel 2:28-32 "And it shall come to pass afterward that I will pour out My Spirit on all flesh; your sons and your daughters shall prophesy, your old men shall dream dreams, your young men shall see visions. And also on *My* menservants and on *My* maidservants, I will pour out My Spirit in those days. And I will show wonders in the heavens and in the earth: Blood and fire and pillars of smoke. The sun shall be turned into darkness, And the moon into blood, Before the coming of the great and awesome day of the LORD. And it shall come to pass *That* whoever calls on the name of the LORD Shall be saved. For in Mount Zion and in Jerusalem there shall be deliverance, As the LORD has said, Among the remnant whom the LORD calls" (2:28-32).

AMOS: THE JUDGMENT OF GOD

Subject The subject of Amos is the judgment of God.

Structure First, there is a series of judgments (chs. 1-2), then a series of sermons (chs. 3-6), and finally, there is a series of visions (chs. 7-9).

I.	Introduction: Judgment is about to Come	1:1-2
II.	Judgments Announced (Eight Judgments)	1:3-2:16
	A. On Three Heathen Neighbors	1:3-10
	B. On Three Kindred Neighbors	1:11-2:3
	C. On the Sister Nation	2:4-5
	D. On Israel	2:6-16
III.	Judgment Amplified (Three Messages)	3:1-6:14
	A. The First Message	3:1-15
	B. The Second Message	4:1-13
	C. The Third Message	5:1-17
	D. The First Woe	5:17-27
	E. The Second Woe	6:1-14
IV.	Judgment Assured (Five Visions)	7:1-9:10
	A. Visions of Locusts, Fire and Plumb Line	7:1-9
	B. The Protest of Amaziah	7:10-17
	C. The Vision of the Fruit Basket	8:1-14
	D. Vision of the Lord by the Altar	9:1-10
V	Conclusion: God will Restore	9:11-15

Author The author was Amos (1:1). The New Testament confirms that. Stephen quotes from Amos (Acts 7:42) and so does James (Acts 15:16). Amos ministered during Uzziah's reign in the South (767-739 BC) and Jeroboam's reign in the North (782-753 BC; see 1:1). Amos also says it was two years before the earthquake (1:1; see also Zech. 14:5). Thus, Amos' ministry was between 760 and 755 BC, toward the latter part of the reign of Jeroboam II. The date of Amos is 760 BC.

Recipient The recipients were the Israelites in the Northern Kingdom. Yet, the message also warns the Israelites in the Southern Kingdom (3:1; 2:4; 5; 6:1).

Purpose The purpose of Amos is to pronounce judgment on Israel and to prophesy the ultimate restoration of Israel. The vast majority of the material concerns judgment. The conclusion deals with restoration (9:11-15).

Summary: The overall message of Amos is God judges the nations surrounding Israel and Israel, but he will restore Israel.

The overall spiritual truth of Amos is a sovereign God will judge sin and ultimately restore Israel.

Amos 3:3 "Can two walk together, unless they are agreed?"

Amos 5:12-15 "For I know your manifold transgressions and your mighty sins: Afflicting the just *and* taking bribes; Diverting the poor *from justice* at the gate. Therefore, the prudent keep silent at that time, For it *is* an evil time. Seek good and not evil, That you may live; So the LORD God of hosts will be with you, As you have spoken. Hate evil, love good; Establish justice in the gate. It may be that the LORD God of hosts Will be gracious to the remnant of Joseph."

Amos 5:24 "But let justice run down like water, and righteousness like a mighty stream."

Amos 8:11 "'Behold, the days are coming,' says the Lord GOD, 'That I will send a famine on the land, Not a famine of bread, nor a thirst for water, but of hearing the words of the LORD.'"

OBADIAH: THE JUDGMENT OF EDOM

Subject The subject of Obadiah is the judgment of Edom (vss.1-2).
Structure The topics covered in the book of Obadiah determine its structure.

I. Introduction: The Nations are called against Edom	1
II. The Destruction of Edom	2-14
A. The Certainty of Edom's Destruction	2-3
B. The Reason for Edom's Destruction	10-14
III. The Deliverance of Israel	15-21
A. The Day of the Lord in all Nations	15-16
B. The Day of the Lord in Israel	17-21

Author The author was Obadiah (vs. 1). Nothing is given but his name. Consequently, nothing is known of his time, his town, or his family. He is an obscure prophet who probably lived in the Southern Kingdom of Judah. The book describes an attack on Jerusalem that could fit several different situations in the history of Israel. There were four significant invasions of Jerusalem in Old Testament times: 1) By the Egyptians (926 BC) in the reign of Rehoboam (1 Kings 14:24-25), 2) By the Philistines and Arabians (848-41 BC) in the reign of Jehoram (2 Chron. 21:16-17), 3) By Israel (790 BC) in the reign of Amaziah (2 Kings 14:13-14), 4) By Babylon (605-586 BC) in the reign of Zedekiah (2 Kings 24-25). Frankly, no one knows for sure to which invasion Obadiah refers. Many scholars choose number 2 because of the place of Obadiah in the canon and because of the lack of reference to the captivity. Assuming that is the case, the date of the book is about 850 BC.

Recipients The recipients of Obadiah were the Israelites living at the time, perhaps, especially those of Jerusalem.

Purpose The purpose of Obadiah is to declare Edom's doom and Israel's deliverance. Obadiah 15-21 deals with the Day of the Lord.

Summary: The overall message of Obadiah is Edom will be destroyed because of her treatment of Israel and Israel will ultimately be delivered.

The overall spiritual truth is God judges those who mistreat Israel (Gen. 12:1-3) and He will ultimately restore Israel.

Obadiah 1:3-4 "The pride of your heart has deceived you, *You* who dwell in the clefts of the rock, Whose habitation is high; *You* who say in your heart, 'Who will bring me down to the ground?' Though you ascend *as* high as the eagle, And though you set your nest among the stars, From there I will bring you down," says the LORD."

Obadiah 1:15 "For the day of the LORD upon all the nations *is* near; as you have done, it shall be done to you; your reprisal shall return upon your own head."

Obadiah 1:21 "Then saviors shall come to Mount Zion To judge the mountains of Esau, And the kingdom shall be the LORD's."

JONAH: THE GRACE OF GOD

Subject The subject of Jonah is the universality of God's grace (4:2, 10-11).

Structure All other prophetic books chiefly consist of prophetic utterances. Jonah records little of his utterance. It is mostly his experience. It is narrative rather than prophecy. Some divide the book into four parts, a few three. Seeing only two (1:2 and 3:1) is probably more accurate.

I.	Jonah's Commission	1:1-2:10
	A. Jonah's Commission	1:1-2
	B. Jonah's Course	1:3
	C. Jonah's Consequences	1:4-17
	D. Jonah's Confession	2:1-10
II.	Jonah's Recommission	3:1-4:11
	A. Jonah's Recommission	3:1-2
	B. Jonah's Compliance	3:3-4
	C. Nineveh's Conversion	3:5-11
	D. Jonah's Complaint	4:1-3
	E. God's Curriculum	4:4-11

Author The author was Jonah (1:1). Apart from that, there is only one other reference to him in the Old Testament (2 Kings 14:25). Jewish tradition says that he was the son of the widow, Elijah raised from the dead (1 Kings 17: 8-24). Jonah lived and ministered under the reign of Jeroboam II (2 Kings 14:25), who ruled 782-753 BC. That was after Elijah's time and just before Amos and Hosea's. So, the date of Jonah is 760 BC. The ministry described in Jonah was to the Gentile city of Nineveh.

Recipients The recipients of the book are not explicitly stated, but there is no doubt that it was written to the Israelites. After all, it is in the Jewish canon!

Purpose The purpose of Jonah is to demonstrate the extent of God's grace and expose the exclusivism of Israel. God's grace extends beyond Israel to all Gentiles. It is universal. The book does not end with God's grace extending to Nineveh. It ends with God educating Jonah, who was angry with God for saving Nineveh. In adding this last chapter, Jonah is exposing the narrowness of himself and his nation.

Summary: The overall message of Jonah is that God's grace is not national; it is universal. The overall spiritual truth is God's grace extends to all who will trust Him.

Jonah 3:1-2 "Now the word of the LORD came to Jonah the second time, saying, 'Arise, go to Nineveh, that great city, and preach to it the message that I tell you.'"

Jonah 4:1-2 "But it displeased Jonah exceedingly, and he became angry. So he prayed to the LORD, and said, "Ah, LORD, was not this what I said when I was still in my country? Therefore I fled previously to Tarshish; for I know that You *are* a gracious and merciful God, slow to anger and abundant in lovingkindness, One who relents from doing harm."

MICAH: SUMMONS TO JUDGMENT

Subject The subject of Micah is a summons to judgment on sin (3:12).
Structure Micah uses the same repeated phrase, "hear," to convey his message (1:2; 3:1; 6:1; 3:9 uses the phrase, but it is a repetition of 3:1). In each section, there is judgment and hope.

I.	Introduction	1:1
II.	Summon to the people	1:2-2:13
	A. Judgment	1:2-2:11
	B. Hope	2:12-13
III.	Summon to the leaders	3:1-5:15
	A. Judgment	3:1-12
	B. Hope	4:1-5:15
IV.	Summon to the mountains	6:1-7:20
	A. Judgment	6:1-16
	B. Hope	7:1-20

Author Micah, who was from the Southern Kingdom, was the author (1:1). He is quoted in Jeremiah 26:17-19. He was a contemporary of Hosea in the North and Isaiah in the South (Isaiah prophesied seventeen or eighteen years before Micah). Isaiah and Micah contain one message in common (*cf.* 4:1-3 with Isa. 2:2-4). Isaiah ministered in the court, Micah to the common man. The dating of Micah is not difficult. Micah lived and lectured in the days of Jotham, Ahaz, and Hezekiah (1:1). Jotham reigned from 750-731 BC, Ahaz from 735-715 BC, and Hezekiah from 715-686 BC. He predicted the fall of Samaria (1:6), which means much of his ministry took place before the Assyrian captivity in 722 BC. His strong denunciation of idolatry and immorality also suggests that his ministry largely preceded the sweeping religious reforms of Hezekiah. So, while he could have ministered from 739-686, the major part of his ministry was probably between 735-710 BC. Micah wrote before 722 BC, perhaps about 725 BC.

Recipients The recipients were both the Southern and the Northern kingdoms. Micah 1:1 says the message concerned Samaria and Jerusalem. Micah, therefore, is the only prophet whose ministry was directed to both kingdoms. The moral conditions during Miach's time were corrupt. No class of people was exempt. Princes, prophets, priests, and people were all victims of social disorder and moral decay (2:2, 8, 9, 11; 3:1-3; 5:11). Yet they clung to religious ordinances and forms. Micah exposes the futility of it all (4:7-8). Micah addresses the Northern Kingdom as if it can still escape divine judgment through last-minute repentance. Jeremiah 26:18-19 indicates that his warnings were taken seriously, and he made an important contribution to the revival under government sponsorship. Ultimately, however, they did not listen. Samaria fell in 722 BC.

Purpose The purpose of Micah is to expose sin, pronounce judgment, and promise hope. They had outward conformity to ritual. God wanted inward conformity to righteousness.

Summary: The overall message of Micah is that God will judge sin, but He will ultimately bless Israel.

The overall spiritual truth is that God judges the sins of His people, but He will ultimately bless them.

Micah 5:2 "But you, Bethlehem Ephrathah, *though* you are little among the thousands of Judah, *Yet* out of you shall come forth to Me The One to be Ruler in Israel, Whose goings forth *are* from of old, From everlasting."

Micah 6:8 "He has shown you, O man, what *is* good; And what does the LORD require of you But to do justly, To love mercy, And to walk humbly with your God?"

Micah 7:18 "Who *is* a God like You, Pardoning iniquity And passing over the transgression of the remnant of His heritage? He does not retain His anger forever, because He delights *in* mercy."

NAHUM: THE JUDGMENT ON NINEVEH

Subject The subject of Nahum is the judgment of Nineveh.

Structure Nahum does not use a literary device to indicate the structure of his thought. The content is the only clue.

I.	Introduction	1:1
II.	Nineveh's Judgment Decreed	1:2-15
	A. The Divine Judge	1:2-7
	B. The Divine Judgment	1:8-15
III.	Nineveh's Judgment Described	2:1-13
	A. The Siege and Capture	2:1-8
	B. The Sacking of the City	2:9-13
IV.	Nineveh's Judgment Deserved	3:1-19
	A. Because of Her Sin	3:1-7
	B. Because of Justice	3:8-19

Author Nahum is the author (1:1). All that is known of him is what is said about him in this verse. It only tells of his town. Nahum 3:8-10 refers to the fall of No-Amon (Thebes). That Egyptian city fell in 664 BC. Nahum predicted the fall of Nineveh, which took place in 612 BC. So, Nahum must be placed somewhere between 664 and 612 BC. No-Amon was restored a decade after its defeat. Nahum's failure to mention that has led to the conclusion that Nahum was written before 654 BC. The date was probably about 655 BC when Nineveh was still in its glory.

Recipients The recipients of Nahum were the Israelites living at the time. The book is *against* Nineveh (1:1), but technically, it is *to* Judah (1:15). Jonah preached to Nineveh about 760 BC. The city was converted, but evidently, the revival was short-lived. The Assyrians soon returned to their ruthless practices. Sargon II of Assyria destroyed Samaria in 722 BC.

Purpose The purpose of Nahum is to condemn Nineveh, vindicate God, and comfort Judah. The Assyrians had defeated the Northern Kingdom in 722 BC. Judah had escaped then, but Assyria was still at the zenith of power. The question in the minds of the Jewish people was, "Would Judah be punished too? Would Assyria conquer Judah?" Nahum brings good news (1:15). Nahum's earnest desire is to see God vindicate His holiness and justice in the eyes of the heathen.

Summary: The overall message of Nahum is that Nineveh will be judged, God will be vindicated, and thus, Israel can be comforted.

The overall spiritual truth is that God comforts His children by informing them that He will judge those who hurt them.

Nahum 1:2 "God *is* jealous, and the LORD avenges; the LORD avenges and *is* furious. The LORD will take vengeance on His adversaries, And He reserves *wrath* for His enemies."

Nahum 1:3 "The LORD *is* slow to anger and great in power, and will not at all acquit *the wicked*. The LORD has His way in the whirlwind and in the storm, and the clouds *are* the dust of His feet."

Nahum 1:7 "The LORD *is* good, a stronghold in the day of trouble; and He knows those who trust in Him."

Assyria and Nineveh were known for their power and cruelty. Most of their gods were gods of war. Nahum describes Nineveh's destruction in detail. It would be destroyed by a flood (1:8, 2:6) and fire (1:10; 2:13; 3:13, 15). The Temples and images would be profaned (1:14). The city would never be rebuilt (1:14, 2:11, 13). The leaders will flee (2:9, 3:17). The fortress around the city will be easily captured (3:12). The gates will be destroyed (3:13) and there will be a lengthy siege and frantic efforts to strengthen its defenses (3:14). Historical accounts and archeological finds have verified that what Nahum predicted is exactly what happened. When Alexander marched by it in 331 BC, there was no evidence of its existence. In the second century AD, not a vestige of it remained. So complete was the destruction of Nineveh that the city was almost a myth for two millennia until its discovery by Layard and Botta in 1842.

HABAKKUK: THE RIGHTEOUSNESS OF GOD

Subject The subject of Habakkuk is the righteousness of God.

Structure The literary structure of the book of Habakkuk is a conversation between Habakkuk and God.

I.	Introduction	1:1
II.	The Prophet's Problems: The Righteousness of God	1:2-2:20
	A. First Problem: Israel's Sin and God's Silence	1:2-11
	B. Second Problem: Babylon's Cruelty and God's Silence	2:12-20
III.	The Prophet's Prayer: The Right Response to a Righteous God	3:1-19

Author Habakkuk is mentioned as the author twice (1:1; 3:1). Beyond that, virtually nothing is known about him except that he was a prophet (1:1; 3:1). He is not mentioned elsewhere in the Bible. There is no explicit time reference in Habakkuk. No king is named in the introduction, but the Babylonian invasion is pictured as imminent (1:6; 2:1; 3:16). The descriptions indicate that Babylon had become a world power. The Chaldeans conquered Babylon in 612 BC, so it had to be after that. It is unlikely that the prophecy took place during the reign of Josiah (640-609 BC) because Josiah's moral and spiritual reforms do not fit the situation in Habakkuk 1:2-4. The prophet's concern for violence in Judah suggests a time after the death of Josiah during the wicked reign of Jehoiakim. The most likely date would be about 607 BC when Jehoiachim's reign was still well underway and before Nebuchadnezzar invaded Judah in 605 BC. Thus, Habakkuk was a contemporary of Jeremiah, prophesying with him in the Southern Kingdom as it plunged toward national collapse.

Recipients The recipients were the Israelites living in the Southern Kingdom. The nobles and even religious leaders were shamelessly robbing and oppressing the common people in Judah. Therefore, they were to be punished through the instrumentality of the Babylonians. In fact, the nobility was the first to be taken into captivity in the two preliminary deportations of 605 and 597 BC. The majority of the lower class was left in the land until the third deportation in 586 BC. Habakkuk sees that the Babylonians pose a serious problem theologically. How is one to reconcile a holy God using them; they were bloody and ruthless people who had no respect for God's moral law? Instead of falling into impatient cynicism, Habakkuk puts the situation before the Lord (2:1). The book is God's answer to Habakkuk.

Purpose The purpose of Habakkuk is to vindicate God's righteousness in using one wicked nation to punish another.

Summary: The overall message of Habakkuk is God is righteous in using a wicked nation to punish another nation.

The overall spiritual truth is that even though it sometimes seems as if God is idle, indifferent, and inconsistent, He is righteous and the right way to respond to Him is to trust Him.

Habakkuk 2:4 "Behold the proud, His soul is not upright in him; But the just shall live by his faith."

Habakkuk 3:2 "O LORD, I have heard Your speech *and* was afraid; O LORD, revive Your work in the midst of the years! In the midst of the years, make *it* known; in wrath, remember mercy."

Habakkuk 3:17-19 "Though the fig tree may not blossom, Nor fruit be on the vines; Though the labor of the olive may fail, And the fields yield no food; Though the flock may be cut off from the fold, And there be no herd in the stalls. Yet I will rejoice in the LORD; I will joy in the God of my salvation. The LORD God is my strength; He will make my feet like deer's *feet,* And He will make me walk on my high hills. To the Chief Musician. With my stringed instruments."

ZEPHANIAH: THE DAY OF THE LORD

Subject The subject of Zephaniah is the Day of the Lord.

Structure Zephaniah is pure preaching (1:2). The Day of the Lord includes judgment and blessing, the Tribulation, and the Millennium. Those are the two aspects of the Day of the Lord and they form the divisions of the book.

I.	Introduction	1:1
II.	The Day of the Lord—Judgment	1:2-3:7
	A. Judgment on Judah and Jerusalem	1:2-2:3
	B. Judgment on the Surrounding Nations	2:4-15
	C. Judgment on Jerusalem	3:1-7
III.	The Day of the Lord—Blessing	3:8-20

Author Zephaniah was the author (1:1). He was thus the only minor prophet of the royal family. Being a distant cousin of King Josiah, Zephaniah had access to the royal court and knew the religious climate around Jerusalem well. Zephaniah dates his book. In Zephaniah 1:1, he speaks of "the days of Josiah." Josiah reigned from 640 BC to 609 BC. Zephaniah 2:13 indicates that the destruction of Nineveh was still in the future. That happened in 612 BC. So, the book must be dated before that. The sins listed in Zephaniah 1:3-13 and 3:1-7 indicate a date before Josiah's reform when the sins for the reign of Manasseh and Amon were still prominent. Zephaniah should be dated around 630-625 BC. Jeremiah, Nahum, and Habakkuk were his contemporaries.

Recipients The recipients were the Israelites living in the Southern Kingdom. The evil reigns of Manasseh and Amon (totaling 55 years) affected Judah so much that it never recovered. Zephaniah probably played a significant role in preparing Judah for the revivals that took place during the reign of the nation's last righteous king. Josiah's reforms were too little too late and the people reverted to their crass idolatry and teaching soon after Josiah was gone. Nevertheless, Zephaniah was one of the eleventh-hour prophets to Judah.

Purpose The simple and single purpose of Zephaniah seems to be to compel Judah to repent. Zephaniah 2:3 is the key verse. To accomplish that purpose, Zephaniah does two things: 1) He announces coming judgment. He announces doom and destruction and urges them to seek the Lord that they "might be hidden in the day of the Lord's anger" (2:3). 2) He announces the coming blessing (3:13). This truth is often neglected or forgotten. The goodness of God also leads to repentance (Rom. 2:4). Evidently, it worked. If Zephaniah prophesied early in the reign of Josiah, he contributed to the revival and reforms under Josiah. It was short-lived, but it worked.

Summary: The overall message of Zephaniah is the Day the Lord is coming and, therefore, Judah should seek the Lord.

The overall spiritual truth is that knowing the Day of the Lord, including a day of judgment and a day of blessing, is coming should cause all to seek the Lord.

Zephaniah 2:3 "Seek the LORD, all you meek of the earth, who have upheld His justice. Seek righteousness, seek humility. It may be that you will be hidden in the day of the LORD's anger."

Zephaniah 3:17 "The LORD your God in your midst, the Mighty One, will save; He will rejoice over you with gladness, He will quiet you with His love, He will rejoice over you with singing."

HAGGAI: THE REBUILDING OF THE TEMPLE

Subject The subject of Haggai is the rebuilding of the Temple (1:2-4, 8, 9, 14; 2:3, 7, 15).

Structure The structure is dated messages. The only difficulty is that some see only four messages, while others see five. The key phrase is "the word of the Lord came."

I.	First Message: Neglecting the Temple	1:1-15
	A. Rebuke for Neglecting the Temple	1:2-4
	B. Results of Neglecting the Temple	1:5-11
	C. Resolve to Rebuild the Temple	1:12-15
II.	Second Message: the Glory of the Temple	2:1-9
	A. The Glory of the Present Temple	2:1-5
	B. The Glory of the Future Temple	2:6-9
III.	Third Message: the Blessing of Rebuilding the Temple	2:10-19
	A. Economic Blight of Neglecting the Temple	2:10-17
	B. Economic Blessing of Building the Temple	2:18, 19
IV.	Fourth Message: the Kingdom is Coming	2:20-23
	A. Future Overthrow of Gentile Kingdoms	2:20-22
	B. Future Authority of Zerubbabel's Kingdom	2:23

Author Haggai is the author (1:1). His name appears nine times (1:1, 1:3, 12, 13; 2:1, 10, 13, 14, 20). He is known only from his book and two references to him in Ezra 5:1 and 6:14. Haggai returned from Babylon with the remnant under Zerubbabel and lived in Jerusalem. Haggai and Zechariah worked together to encourage the people to rebuild the Temple. Haggai is one of the most precisely dated books in the Bible: Haggai 1:1 (August 29, 520 BC), Haggai 1:15 (September 21, 520 BC), Haggai 2:1 (October 17, 520 BC), Haggai 2:20 (December 18, 520 BC). In other words, this book spans four months. After fourteen years of neglect, work was resumed in 520 BC. By the way, the Temple was completed in 516 BC (Ezra 6:15).

Recipients The recipients were the Israelites who returned after the captivity. Zerubbabel led the first return in 536 BC and began work on the Temple (Ezra 4-6). The people were soon discouraged by the desolation of the land, crop failure, hard work, and even hostility from their neighbors. Their work on the Temple ceased in 534 BC. The people became preoccupied with their own building projects. They used political opposition and a theory that the Temple was not to be rebuilt until sometime later (perhaps after Jerusalem was rebuilt) as excuses for neglecting the Temple. God then called Haggai and Zechariah to convince the people to complete the Temple. The recipients were Zerubbabel, the governor; Joshua, the High Priest (1:1; 2:2, 21); and all the people (1:13; 2:2).

Purpose The purpose of Haggai is to encourage the people to rebuild the Temple and to enlighten them as to God's blessing. Putting their self-interests first led to dissatisfaction. Only when they put God first and sought to do His will would He bring His people joy and prosperity.

Summary: The overall message is the people and the leaders of Israel need to rebuild the Temple in particular and be obedient in general (1:12).

The overall spiritual truth is joy and blessing come from putting God and His work first.

Haggai 1:5 "Now, therefore, thus says the LORD of hosts: "Consider your ways!"

Haggai 2:9 "The glory of this latter temple shall be greater than the former,' says the LORD of hosts. 'And in this place I will give peace,' says the LORD of hosts."

ZECHARIAH: THE FUTURE OF JERUSALEM

Subject The subject of Zechariah is the restoration of Jerusalem (1:16; 2:2; 8:3; 9:9; 12:5; 13:1; 14:2).

Structure The literary structure of Zechariah 1:7-6:8 is a series of visions (1:8, 18; 2:1; 3:1, etc.). In Zechariah 6:9-8:23, he says, "The word of the Lord came unto me." Chapters 7 and 8 contain questions. The last chapters, Zechariah 9-14, consist of two "burdens" (9:1 and 12:1).

I.	Introduction: A Call to Repentance	1:1-6
II.	Visions: Israel's Future	1:7-6:15
III.	Questions: Fasting and Israel's Future	7:1 - 8:23
	A. Questions about Fasting	7:1-3
	B. The Four-Fold Answer	7:4-8:23
IV.	Burdens: Sherperd's and Israel's Future	9:1-14:21
	A. First Burden	9:1-11:17
	B. Second Burden	12:1-14:21

Author Zechariah was the author (1:1). There are at least twenty-nine men named Zechariah in the Old Testament. This Zechariah was born in Babylon. He was evidently of the priestly lineage (1:1, 7; Ezra 5:1; 6:14; Neh. 12:4, 16), but the book calls him a prophet (1:1, 7). When the Jewish exiles returned under Zerubbabel, Zechariah was among them. He was murdered between the Temple (Mt. 23:35) and the altar, the same way that an earlier man named Zechariah was martyred (see 2 Chron. 24:20-21). Zechariah 1:1 gives the exact date ("In the eighteenth month of the second year of Darius"), November 20, 520 BC. Zechariah was a younger contemporary of Haggai, the prophet, Zerubbabel, the Governor, and Joshua, the High Priest. Haggai began his ministry first (by two months), but their combined preaching resulted in the Temple's completion in 516 BC. The last dated prophecy was in December 518 BC (7:1-8:23). Some have dated it December 4, but chapters 9-14 are not dated and should be put much later, probably about 480 BC. Thus, Zechariah had a 40+ year ministry dating from 520-480 BC.

Recipients The recipients were the Israelites who returned from the captivity (1:2, 4; 7:5; etc.). Some messages were especially addressed to Joshua, the High Priest (3:8), and Zerubbabel, the governor (4:6).

Purpose: The purpose of Zechariah is to stimulate the completion of the Temple by proclaiming the restoration of Jerusalem and to promote spiritual revival so the people would call upon the Lord with humble hearts and commit their ways to Him.

Summary: The overall message is that the people are urged to rebuild the Temple and recommit themselves to the Lord.

The overall spiritual truth is God encourages and renews His people so that they will do His work.

Zechariah 1:3 "Therefore say to them, 'Thus says the LORD of hosts: 'Return to Me,' says the LORD of hosts, "and I will return to you," says the LORD of hosts.?"

Zechariah 2:8 "For thus says the LORD of hosts: 'He sent Me after glory, to the nations which plunder you; for he who touches you touches the apple of His eye.'"

Zechariah 4:6 "So he answered and said to me: 'This *is* the word of the LORD to Zerubbabel: 'Not by might nor by power, but by My Spirit,' Says the LORD of hosts.'"

Zechariah 14:9 "And the LORD shall be King over all the earth. In that day, it shall be 'The LORD *is* one, and His name one.'"

In a sense, Zechariah is continuing the ministry of Haggai to get the Temple completed. Yet he and Haggai approach the goal differently. Haggai uses rebuke, whereas Zechariah employs encouragement. Haggai's chief task was to arouse the people to the necessity of the outward task for rebuilding the Temple, whereas Zechariah goes beyond that to seek an inward spiritual renewal of the people. Zechariah was interested in the physical rebuilding of the Temple and the spiritual renewal of the people.

MALACHI: THE CHARGES OF GOD

Subject The subject of Malachi is God's charges against His people.

Structure Malachi contains a series of God's accusations against Israel: 1) You have doubted My love (1:2). 2) You have despised My name (1:6). 3) You have disobeyed My law (2:14). 4) You have discredited My promise (2:17). 5) You have defrauded My storehouse (3:7, 8). 6) You have denied My blessings (3:13). These are followed by questions, supposedly asked by the audience but stated by the author. These questions are then answered. Two are used in the same charge. Of the fifty-five verses in Malachi, twenty-seven are spoken by God, the highest proportion of all the prophets.

I. Introduction	1:1
II. The Charge against the Nation	1:2-5
III. The Charge against the Priests	1:6-2:9
IV. The Charge against the People	2:10-4:3
V. Conclusion	4:4-6

Author The author was Malachi (1:1). He is only mentioned in this verse. It reveals nothing about him, not even his father's name. All that is known is that Jewish tradition says he was a member of the great synagogue. Malachi is attested by the New Testament (*cf.* Mal. 4:5, 6 with Mt. 11:10, 14, 17:11, 12, Mk. 9:10, 11, and Lk. 1:17; also *cf.* Mal. 3:1 with Mt. 11:10, and Mk 1:2; and Mal. 2, 3 with Rom. 9:13). Malachi 1:1 does not mention his father, his hometown, or the king or kings who reigned during his ministry. Therefore, an exact date cannot be established. However, internal clues help fix an appropriate date: 1) The Edomites had been driven from Mt. Seir but had not returned, necessitating a date after 585 BC (1:3-4). 2) The remnant had returned, rebuilt the Temple, and they were offering sacrifices (1:7-10; 3:8). The Temple was completed in 516 BC, so the book must have been written after that. 3) many years had passed since the offerings were instituted because the priest had grown tired of them and corruption had crept into the system. 4) The moral and religious problems in Malachi are quite similar to those faced by Ezra and Nehemiah. 5) The Persian term for governor (*pechah*) is used in Malachi 1:8. By itself, all this indicates is that the book was written during the Persian domination of Israel (539-333 BC), but the verse indicates that this governor might be bribed. That would hardly be Nehemiah. Nehemiah returned to Persia in 433 BC but returned to Palestine around 420 BC and dealt with the sins described in Malachi. Therefore, it is likely that Malachi proclaimed his message while Nehemiah was absent, almost a century after Haggai and Zechariah began their ministries (520 BC). All this leads to a date of about 430 BC.

Recipients The recipients were the people of Israel (1:1; 2:11; 3:6-7), the priests (1:6, 2:1), and a faithful group (4:2, 3).

Purpose The purpose of Malachi is to rebuke the sins of the priests and the people so that they would return to the Lord.

Summary: The overall message of Malachi is that God rebuked the sins of the priests and the people so that they would return to the Lord (3:7).

The overall spiritual truth is that God rebukes sin to get His people to turn to Him.

Malachi 3:1 "'Behold, I send My messenger, And he will prepare the way before Me. And the Lord, whom you seek, Will suddenly come to His temple, Even the Messenger of the covenant, In whom you delight. Behold, He is coming,' Says the LORD of hosts."

Malachi 3:6 "For I *am* the LORD, I do not change; Therefore you are not consumed, O sons of Jacob."

Malachi 4:5-6 "Behold, I will send you Elijah the prophet Before the coming of the great and dreadful day of the LORD. And he will turn The hearts of the fathers to the children, And the hearts of the children to their fathers, Lest I come and strike the earth with a curse."

MATTHEW: THE KINGSHIP OF JESUS CHRIST

Subject The subject of Matthew is Jesus Christ as Messiah, King of Israel. He is "the Son of David" (1:1, 1:20; 9:27; 12:23; 15:22; 20:30-31; 21:9, 15; 22:45). The Magi seek the "King of the Jews" (2:2). The prophecy of Micah 5:2 is applied to Him (2:6). He is said to fulfill many prophecies and He is called the King (21:5; 27:37).

Structure Five discourses dominate the book (60% of Matthew's 1,071 verses contain the spoken words of Jesus): 1) The Sermon on the Mount (chs 5-7), 2) The Charge to the Twelve (ch 10), 3) The Parables of the Kingdom (ch 13), 4) The Teaching on Greatness and Forgiveness (ch 18), 5) The Olivet Discourse (chs 24-25). With slight variation, each of these discourses ends with the phrase, "Now it came to pass when Jesus had finished these sayings" (7:28; 11:1; 13:53; 19:1; 26:1). While not exactly the marker of the structure of the book, these discourses are a major part of this book. In the final analysis, the subjects covered in the book determine its structure. The book is not in chronological order.

I. Preparation of the King	1:1-7:29
A. His Person	1:1-2:23
B. His Preparation	3:1-4:11
C. His Principles	4:12-7:29
II. Power of the King	8:1-11:1
A. His Miracles	8:1-9:30
B. His Mandate	10:1-11:1
III. Opposition to the King	11:2-13:53
A. The Evidence of Rejection	11:2-30
B. The Illustration of Opposition	12:1-58
C. The Adaptation because of Opposition	13:1-53
IV. Reaction of King	13:54-19:2
A. Withdrawal	13:54-16:12
B. Instruction	16:13-19:2
V. Rejection of the King	19:3-26:1
A. Instruction	19:3-20:34
B. Presentation to the Nation	21:1-17
C. Rejection by the Nation	21:18-22:46
D. Rejection by Christ	23:1-39
E. Prediction by the King	24:1-26:1
VI. Death and Resurrection of the King	26:2-28:20
A. Crucifixion of the King	26:2-27:66
B. Resurrection of the King	28:1-20

Author The author is anonymous. The early writers of the church unanimously credit it to Matthew. Eusebius quotes Papias (ca. 95-110 AD) as saying Matthew composed the logia in

Aramaic. If Matthew wrote in Aramaic, he later wrote in Greek. Only the Greek edition of Matthew has survived. Tradition says after 15 years of preaching in Palestine, Matthew departed for foreign nations but left behind his Hebrew (Aramaic) Gospel. This would give a date of roughly 45 AD for the Aramaic Gospel of Matthew. Matthew wrote before 70 AD. He refers to Jerusalem as "the Holy City" as though it was still standing (4:5; 27:53). He refers to Jewish customs continuing "to this day" (27:8; 28:15). Thus, Matthew was probably written from Syria, Antioch, or Palestine about 45-50 AD. Matthew wrote to Jewish believers to demonstrate that Jesus was the Old Testament Messiah. There are indications that these Jewish believers were undergoing persecution. The purpose of Matthew is to explain that even though Jesus was proven by prophecies to be the Messiah/King, Israel rejected Him, so the kingdom was postponed and to encourage persecuted Jewish Christians in their faith.

Recipients The recipients were Jewish believers who had to explain why Jesus, the Messiah, was rejected and what happened to the kingdom.

Purpose The purpose of Matthew is to demonstrate that Jesus is the Messiah and to explain that the kingdom is postponed. Matthew repeatedly that Jesus fulfilled the Old Testament prophecies and promises concerning the Messiah. He uses more Old Testament quotes and allusions (about 130) than any other book. Matthew also deals with the kingdom issue. He refers to the kingdom of heaven 33 times, but that expression does not occur anywhere else in the New Testament. He first shows that when they rejected their king, the Jews rejected an earthly kingdom (21:28-22:10; 11:16-24). Then, He shows that His kingdom is postponed. The promises of Israel are not canceled; they will be fulfilled (19:28; 20:20-23; 23-39; 24:29-31; 25:31-46).

Summary: The overall message is that Jesus is the Christ, the king of Israel, who was rejected, who died and rose and commissioned His disciples to make disciples among all nations.

The overall spiritual truth is if the Messiah, the King, was rejected, His followers will be too.

Matthew 4:19 "Then He said to them, 'Follow Me, and I will make you fishers of men.'"
Matthew 5-7 The Sermon on the Mount, including the Lord's prayer
Matthew 5:20 "For I say to you, that unless your righteousness exceeds *the righteousness* of the scribes and Pharisees, you will by no means enter the kingdom of heaven."
Matthew 6:33 "But seek first the kingdom of God and His righteousness, and all these things shall be added to you."
Matthew 11:28-30 "Come to Me, all *you* who labor and are heavy laden, and I will give you rest. Take My yoke upon you and learn from Me, for I am gentle and lowly in heart, and you will find rest for your souls. For My yoke *is* easy and My burden is light."
Matthew 13:1-9, 18-23 The Parable of the Sower
Matthew 16:16 "Simon Peter answered and said, 'You are the Christ, the Son of the living God.'"
Matthew 24-25 The Olivet Discourse
Matthew 24:29-30, 25:31 "Immediately after the tribulation of those days the sun will be darkened, and the moon will not give its light; the stars will fall from heaven, and the powers of the heavens will be shaken. Then the sign of the Son of Man will appear in heaven, and then all the tribes of the earth will mourn, and they will see the Son of Man coming on the clouds of heaven with power and great glory…. When the Son of Man comes in His glory, and all the holy angels with Him, then He will sit on the throne of His glory."
Matthew 28:18-20 The Great Commission

MARK: THE SERVANTHOOD OF JESUS CHRIST

Subject The subject of Mark is Jesus Christ as a servant (Mk. 10:45).

Structure Unlike Matthew, Mark is in chronological order. The only other thing that can be said concerning its overall structure is that it is geographical. The emphasis in Mark is on works, not words. There are only a few discourses and only four of the 15 parables of Matthew are given. Jesus is pictured as a worker hastening from one task to another. The word "immediately" occurs over three dozen times. It appears seven times in Matthew and only once in Luke. In Mark's Gospel, 14 of these are used for the personal activity of Jesus as compared to two in Matthew and none in Luke.

I.	Introduction	1:1-13
II.	The Servant's Ministry in Galilee (to minister)	1:14-9:50
III.	The Servant's Ministry in Judah	10:1-52
IV.	The Servant's Ministry in Jerusalem (to give His life)	11:1-13:37
V.	Conclusion: The Servant's Death and Resurrection	14:1-16:20

Author The author is not mentioned by name. There is early evidence that John Mark wrote the Gospel of Mark. Papias writes that the apostle John said Mark wrote Peter's words. Mark was written before the destruction of Jerusalem, which occurred in 70 AD (13:2). Beyond that, little is known. Even tradition disagrees as to whether it was written before or after the martyrdom of Peter. Clement of Alexandria says, "The Romans entreated Mark to record Peter's preaching." If so, the Gospel of Mark was written during his close association with Peter in Rome between 61 and 67 AD (Col. 4:10).

Recipients The recipients were the believers in Rome. Mark wrote for Roman readers: 1) The book only somewhat emphasizes Jewish law and customs. 2) Latinisms are often used where Greek terms could have served (4:21; 6:27; 12:14, 42; 15:15; 16:39). 3) Aramaic words are interpreted (3:17; 5:41; 7:34, 15:22). 4) The style is terse, clear, and pointed. 5) Mark 15:21 mentions Simon the Cyrenian, the father of Alexander and Rufus. If this is the same Rufus as the one mentioned in Romans 16:13, there is a strong indication that Roman Christians are being addressed here. 6) Antiquity is unanimous in affirming that Mark wrote to Roman readers. 7) Mark, rather than Matthew, Luke, or John, corresponds to Peter's address at Caesarea (Acts 10:34-43).

Purpose The purpose of Mark is to present Jesus Christ as the Son of God who came to give His life in service and suffering and, thus, encourage Roman Christians in their service and suffering. While Mark stresses the servanthood of Jesus, he does not neglect the Sonship of Jesus Christ (1:1). This Servant is the Son of God!

Summary: The overall message of Mark is that Jesus is the Son of God who came to serve, die for sin, be resurrected, and commission His disciples to preach the gospel to the entire world.

The overall spiritual truth is servants give their lives away, serving others, and they suffer. That is what Jesus did; that is what we are to do (Eph. 5:24; Phil. 2:17).

Mark 4:13 "And He said to them, "Do you not understand this parable? How, then, will you understand all the parables?"

Mark 9:23 "Jesus said to him, 'If you can believe, all things *are* possible to him who believes.'"

Mark 10:23 "Then Jesus looked around and said to His disciples, "How hard it is for those who have riches to enter the kingdom of God!"

Mark 11:24 "Therefore I say to you, whatever things you ask when you pray, believe that you receive *them,* and you will have *them.*"

Mark 10:45 "For even the Son of Man did not come to be served, but to serve, and to give His life a ransom for many."

Mark 12:29-31 "Jesus answered him, 'The first of all the commandments *is*: 'Hear, O Israel, the Lord our God, the Lord is one. and you shall love the Lord your God with all your heart, with all your soul, with all your mind, and with all your strength.' This *is* the first commandment. and the second, like *it, is* this: 'you shall love your neighbor as yourself.' There is no other commandment greater than these.'"

Mark 14:38 "Watch and pray, lest you enter into temptation. The spirit indeed *is* willing, but the flesh *is* weak."

Mark 16:15-20 The Great Commission

The backdrop of Mark is Nero's persecution of Christians. Roman Christians found in the Gospel of Mark that what they suffered from Nero was like the experience of Jesus. Only Mark records that in the wilderness, Jesus was with the wild beasts (1:13). That had special significance for those called to enter the arena while they stood helpless in the presence of wild beasts. Likewise, Jesus had been misrepresented to the people and falsely labeled (3:21-30). If an intimate friend had betrayed them, it was sobering to know that one of the twelve had been Judas Iscariot, who had also betrayed Jesus (13:19).

Mark records that Jesus says, "Those who have no root in themselves but endure for a while, then after affliction or persecution arises on account of this world, immediately they fall away" (4:17). While Jesus promised His followers "houses and brothers and sisters and mothers and children and lands," Mark notes that He had added the qualification "with persecutions" (10:30). Jesus spoke of cross-bearing, which Tacitus affirms was a literal reality for Mark's readers in Rome. Such had been the literal experience of Jesus preceded by a trial before a Roman magistrate, which included scourging and cruel mockery of the Roman guard (15:15-20). The threat of such punishment could move a man to deny Jesus. The explicit reference to Peter meant that the way was open for restoration for one who had denied the Lord (14:66-72). Here is the basis for forgiveness for those who had denied that they were Christians when brought before the Tribunals of Rome. The situation in Rome was such that they would have read the Gospel in this light.

LUKE: THE HUMANITY OF JESUS CHRIST

Subject The subject of Luke is Jesus Christ as the Son of Man.

Structure The literary structure of Luke, like Matthew and Mark, is topical yet geographical. Luke has a repeated phrase in one section. Matthew and Mark devote only a short space (two chapters in Matthew and one in Mark) for the journey from Galilee to Jerusalem. In contrast, Luke spends ten chapters chronicling that trip, the longest part of his story (9:51-19:44).

I.	Preface	1:1-4
II.	The Preparation for the Son of Man	1:5-4:13
III	The Galilean Ministry of the Son of Man	4:14-9:50
IV.	The Journey to Jerusalem of the Son of Man	9:51-19:20
V.	The Jerusalem Ministry of the Son of Man	19:21-21:38
VI.	The Passion and Resurrection of the Son of Man	22:1-24:53

Author The author is anonymous. From the earliest times, Luke has been universally recognized as the author. Luke says, 1) Many have written a narrative of the life and ministry of Jesus (1:1; these were *written* sources). 2) His information came from "eyewitnesses and ministers of the Word." (1:2). These were *oral* sources. In the Greek text, there is only one article indicating one group. 3) He had a perfect understanding of all things from the first (1:3). Luke was written before the book of Acts (Acts 1:1-3), which was written about 62 AD. Many have concluded that Luke wrote his Gospel toward the end of Paul's imprisonment in Caesarea, about 59 AD. For those two years, Luke interviewed eyewitnesses throughout Palestine.

Recipients The recipients were Theophilus and Gentiles. Luke addresses his first volume to "most excellent Theophilus" (1:3), a common name among Jews and Gentiles. The epitaph "most excellent" was an official title (Acts 23:26; 24:3; 26:25). Beyond that, nothing is known of him. He was a believer who needed instruction and confirmation. In Greek, the preface (1:1-4) is written in a classical style, which implies that what follows is meant for circulation. The content indicates it was written for Gentiles in general and for Greeks in particular. The genealogy of Christ is traced to Adam, not Abraham. Gentile words are used in place of Jewish terms, for example, "teacher" for "rabbi," "lawyer" for "scribe," etc. Jewish customs and geography are explained. Matthew wrote to the Jews. Mark wrote to the Romans and Luke to the Greeks.

Purpose The purpose is stated in Luke 1:1-4. Luke wrote that Theophilus and other Gentile believers might "know the certainty of those things in which you were instructed." Luke and Acts are a two-volume set. Luke wrote Acts to defend Christianity from political charges. Perhaps that is part of what is going on here. He records Pilate's acknowledgment of Jesus's innocence three times (23:4, 14, and 22). So, another purpose of Luke is to show that Christianity was not a subversive political sect.

Summary: The overall message is Jesus is the Son of Man who came to seek the lost, die, be raised, and commission His disciples to preach the forgiveness of sins.

The overall spiritual truth is that the followers of the Son of Man should, like Him, seek to save those who are lost.

Luke 2:14 "Glory to God in the highest, And on earth peace, goodwill toward men!"
Luke 4:1-13 The Temptation of Christ
Luke 5:32 "I have not come to call *the* righteous, but sinners, to repentance."
Luke 14:25-35 The Cost of Discipleship
Luke 19:10 "For the Son of Man has come to seek and to save that which was lost."
Luke 21:33 "Heaven and earth will pass away, but My words will by no means pass away."
Luke 10:25-27 The Parable of the Good Samaritan
Luke 15:11-32 The Parable of the Prodigal Son
Luke 24:44-49 "Then He said to them, 'These *are* the words which I spoke to you while I was still with you, that all things must be fulfilled which were written in the Law of Moses and *the* Prophets and *the* Psalms concerning Me.' And He opened their understanding, that they might comprehend the Scriptures. Then He said to them, 'Thus it is written, and thus it was necessary for the Christ to suffer and to rise from the dead the third day, and that repentance and remission of sins should be preached in His name to all nations, beginning at Jerusalem. And you are witnesses of these things. Behold, I send the Promise of My Father upon you; but tarry in the city of Jerusalem until you are endued with power from on high.'"

Luke presents Jesus Christ as perfect humanity, the ideal man. Luke does not minimize Jesus' deity or His suffering, but he focuses on the humanity of Jesus, who was the Son of Man, as well as the Son of God. A proper assessment of Jesus must include both His divine and human natures. The particulars paint the picture of Jesus' humanity: 1) Luke puts Jesus in the context of history. Three times in the early chapters, Luke notes political rulers at the moment (1:5; 2:1; 3:1), again putting the story in historical perspective. 2) The genealogy traces Jesus' lineage to Adam (3:38). 3) Luke alone records Jesus' human growth and development (2:40, 51, 52). He was subject to his parents (2:52). 4) Throughout the book, Jesus is seen as having the feelings, sympathies, and powers of a man. He rejoiced in the Holy Spirit (10:21). He wept over the city (19:41). He prayed earnestly and sweat great drops of blood (22:44).

Luke wrote to the Greeks. The Greek ideal of perfect manliness differed from that of the Romans. The Romans felt that it was their mission to govern. The Greeks felt it theirs to educate, elevate, and perfect man. The ideal of the Romans was military glory and governmental authority, but the Greeks' ideal was wisdom and beauty. The perfect man died for imperfect men (19:10).

JOHN: THE DEITY OF JESUS CHRIST

Subject The subject of John is Jesus as the Christ, the Son of God.

Structure The structure is chronological and geographical. John chooses "witnesses" to testify to the deity and Messiahship of Jesus.

I. Prologue	1:1-18
II. Witnesses During His Public Ministry	1:19-12:50
A. Witnesses During the Call of the Disciples	1:19-2:11
B. Witnesses During the Commencement of His Ministry	2:12-4:54
C. Witnesses During the Controversy	5:1-6:71
D. Witnesses During the Conflict	7:1-10:42
E. Witnesses During the Climax	11:1-12:50
III Witnesses During His Private Ministry	13:1-17:26
A. Witnesses of the Foot Washing	13:1-30
B. Witness of His Announced Departure	13:31-14:41
C. Witness of the Discourse on Relationships	15:1-16:6
D. Witness of the Discourse of Why He Was Leaving	16:7-33
E. Witness of the Lord's Prayer	17:1-26
IV. Witnesses During the Passion	18:1-20:31
A. Witnesses During the Arrest and Trial	18:1-27
B. Witnesses During the Trial Before Pilate	18:28-19:15
C. Witnesses During the Crucifixion	19:16-42
D. Witnesses During His Appearance	20:1-31
V. Epilogue	21:1-25

Author The author of the fourth Gospel identifies himself, but not by name. In John 21:19-24, he refers to himself as the disciple whom Jesus loved (that phrase occurs five times: 13:23; 19:26; 20:2; 21:7; 21:20). In the Upper Room, where only the apostles were present, the disciple whom Jesus loved was leaning on Jesus' breast (21:20). Hence, he had to have been one of the apostles. In addition, the "one whom Jesus loved" was part of the inner circle of Peter, James, and John (Mt. 10:2; 17:1; Gal. 2:9). It was not Peter. In the Upper Room, Peter asked the one whom Jesus loved, the one leaning on Jesus' breast, a question. Only James and John are left. James was martyred too early to be the author (Acts 12:1-2). That leaves John. Furthermore, when referred to in the book, John is never called by name (1:40; 13:23; 21:20, 24), but all the other Gospel writers name him. Therefore, the apostle John must be the author of the fourth Gospel. Tradition confirms that conclusion. Polycarp, a disciple of John, had a disciple named Irenaeus (ca. 185 AD). In his book against heresies, Irenaeus says, "John wrote a gospel." Others also ascribe the book to John. The Gospel of John was written before 70 A.D. John 5:2 indicates that Jerusalem had not yet been destroyed. That verse says, "Which is (present tense) in Jerusalem." There is an early and consistent tradition that John wrote from Ephesus at the request of the church for a summary of his oral teachings on the life of Jesus. Eusebius refers to a current opinion that John wrote after the other evangelists to supply an account of the early period of the Lord's ministry, which they omitted.

Recipients No particular readers are specified. The whole world is in view (1:9-12; 3:16, 17-18; 21:23).

Purpose The major purpose of the Gospel of John is evangelistic; the minor purposes are to strengthen the faith of believers and urge them to become disciples. John, records signs that his readers may believe that Jesus is the Christ, the Son of God and that by believing, they may have life in His name (20:31). Thus, his primary purpose is evangelistic, but since all seven signs appear in the first half of the book (2:1-11; 4:46-54; 5:1-18; 6:5-14; 6:16-21; 9:1-7; 11:1-45; in 20:30 the resurrection is also called a sign), there must be other purposes. Several statements in the book indicate the intent of the author is to strengthen the faith of those who already believe (2:11; 11:4; 11:15; 11:40-42; 13:19; 14:29; 16:30). There are also passages dealing with discipleship (8:30-32; 13:1-17; 13:34-35; 14:12-26; 15:1-16:15; 17:26; 20:19-23; 19:24-29; 21:1-19).

Summary: The overall message of John is Jesus is the Messiah/Son of God who came to give eternal life to all who believe in Him, to die, be raised, and commission His disciples to proclaim the gift of eternal life.

The overall spiritual truth is those who believe in Jesus Christ for eternal life *have* eternal life, and if they continue in His Word, they are His disciples.

John 3:16 "For God so loved the world that He gave His only begotten Son, that whoever believes in Him should not perish but have everlasting life."

John 3:36 "He who believes in the Son has everlasting life; and he who does not believe the Son shall not see life, but the wrath of God abides on him."

John 5:24 "Most assuredly, I say to you, he who hears My word and believes in Him who sent Me has everlasting life, and shall not come into judgment, but has passed from death into life."

John 8:31 "Then Jesus said to those Jews who believed Him, 'If you abide in My word, you are My disciples indeed.'"

John 8:32 "And you shall know the truth, and the truth shall make you free."

John 10:28 "And I give them eternal life, and they shall never perish; neither shall anyone snatch them out of My hand."

John 13:34 "A new commandment I give to you, that you love one another; as I have loved you, that you also love one another."

John 14:6 "Jesus said to him, 'I am the way, the truth, and the life. No one comes to the Father except through Me.'"

John 14:21 "He who has My commandments and keeps them, it is he who loves Me. And he who loves Me will be loved by My Father, and I will love him and manifest Myself to him."

John 14:23 "Jesus answered and said to him, 'If anyone loves Me, he will keep My word; and My Father will love him, and We will come to him and make Our home with him.'"

John 15:5 "I am the vine, you *are* the branches. He who abides in Me, and I in him, bears much fruit; for without Me you can do nothing."

John 16:7 "Nevertheless I tell you the truth. It is to your advantage that I go away; for if I do not go away, the Helper will not come to you; but if I depart, I will send Him to you."

ACTS: THE SPREAD OF CHRISTIANITY

Subject The subject of Acts is the continuing work of Jesus Christ (see "and" in Acts 1:1).

Structure Acts 1:8 lays out the structure geographically: Jerusalem (chs. 1-7), Judea/Samaria (chs. 8-12), and uttermost parts (chs. 13-28). There is also a deliberate structuring of the material around the acts of Peter (chs. 1-12) and the acts of Paul (chs. 13-28).

I. The Lord's Work by the Holy Spirit through the Men in Jerusalem	1:1-7:60
II. The Lord's Work by the Holy Spirit through the Men in Judea and Samaria	8:1-12:25
III. The Lord's Work by the Holy Spirit through the Men to the Uttermost Parts of the Earth	13:1-28:31

Author The author's name is not given, but the first verse refers to the former treatise sent to Theophilus. Luke wrote his Gospel to Theophilus. Therefore, he is the author of Acts. Luke traveled with Paul (see the "we" sections, 16:10-17; 20:5-21:18; 27:1-28:16). Therefore, he had access to eyewitnesses of events recorded in chapters 13-28. Perhaps he interviewed key witnesses in Jerusalem, such as Peter and John, for the information in chapters 1-12. He may have used written sources as well (15:23-29 and 23:26-30). Luke abruptly ends the book with Paul waiting for his trial in Rome. Acts gives nothing of the persecution under Nero in 64 AD, Paul's death in 68 AD, or the destruction of Jerusalem in 70 AD. So, since Paul came to Rome about 59 AD and had been there for two years when Acts closed, the book can confidently be dated 61 AD. It was written to Theophilus, a Gentile government official and Christian, but it is not a personal letter. It is a formal treatise intended for publication.

Recipients The recipients were Theophilus and Gentiles in general.

Purpose The purposes of Acts were to chronicle the spread of the work inaugurated by Jesus, which He continued by the Holy Spirit through the men from Jerusalem to Rome and to defend Paul. Paul did what Peter, an apostle of Jesus, did. Peter preached, resulting in conversions (2:14-41). Paul preached, resulting in conversions (13:16-43, 14:8-20, etc.). Peter healed a lame man (3:1-10). Paul healed a lame man (14:8-10). Peter raised Tabitha (Dorcas) from the dead (9:36-42). Paul raised Eutychus from the dead (20:7-12). Peter healed people when his shadow passed over them (5:15-16). Paul healed people when they were touched by his handkerchiefs and aprons (19:11-12). Peter survived an encounter with a venomous snake (28:3-6). Paul survived an encounter with a venomous snake (28:3-6). Peter was miraculously released from prison (12:1-11). Paul was miraculously released from prison (16:22-34; 23:23-35; 27:21-28:6). Peter preached to Gentiles (ch. 10). Paul preached to Gentiles (13:46-48; 18:6; 22:21; etc.). Thus, Paul was not a traitor to his people, an apostate from the law, or an insurrectionist; like Peter, he was an instrument in the hand of God.

Summary: The overall message is Jesus Christ continued His work by the Holy Spirit through men, especially Peter and Paul, from the Jews in Jerusalem to the Gentiles in Rome.

The overall spiritual truth believers are to bear witness of Jesus Christ in the power of the Holy Spirit, beginning where they are and from there to the ends of the earth (Acts 1:8).

Acts 1:5 "For John truly baptized with water, but you shall be baptized with the Holy Spirit not many days from now."

Acts 1:8 "But you shall receive power when the Holy Spirit has come upon you; and you shall be witnesses to Me in Jerusalem, and in all Judea and Samaria, and to the end of the earth."

Acts 4:12 "Nor is there salvation in any other, for there is no other name under heaven given among men by which we must be saved."

Acts 5:29 "But Peter and the *other* apostles answered and said: 'We ought to obey God rather than men.'"

Acts 10:43 "To Him all the prophets witness that, through His name, whoever believes in Him will receive remission of sins."

Acts 16:31 "So they said, 'Believe on the Lord Jesus Christ, and you will be saved, you and your household.'

Acts 20:24 "But none of these things move me; nor do I count my life dear to myself, so that I may finish my race with joy, and the ministry which I received from the Lord Jesus, to testify to the gospel of the grace of God."

Acts 20:28 "Therefore take heed to yourselves and to all the flock, among which the Holy Spirit has made you overseers, to shepherd the church of God which He purchased with His own blood."

ROMANS: THE RIGHTEOUSNESS OF GOD

Subject The subject of Romans is the righteousness of God.
Structure The literary structure of Romans is in the format of an ancient letter, which had a salutation, thanksgiving, prayer, body, personal greetings, and benediction.

I. Salutation	1:1-7
II. Thanksgiving and Prayer	1:8-17
III. The Body of the Letter	1:18-15:13
A. Righteousness Needed	1:18-3:20
1. All are under Condemnation	1:18-32
2. The Jews are under Condemnation	2:1-3:8
3. Conclusion: All are Condemned	3:9-20
B. Righteousness imputed	3:21-5:11
1. Justification by Faith Explained	3:21-31
2. Justification by Faith Illustrated	4:1-25
3. Justification by Faith Enjoyed	5:1-11
C. Righteous Accomplished	5:12-8:39
1. Justification to Life	5:12-21
2. First Objection	6:1-14
3. Second Objection	6:15-7:6
4. Third Objection	7:7-25
5. The Solution	8:1-39
D. Righteousness Vindicated	9:1-11:36
1. Israel Past: Election	9:1-29
2. Israel Present: Rejection	9:30-10:21
3. Israel Future: Salvation	11:1-36
E. Righteousness Practiced	12:1-15:13
1. In the Church	12:1-8
2. In Society	12:9-21
3. Toward Government	13:1-14
4. Toward Other Believers	14:1-15:13
IV. Paul's Plans	15:14-33
V. Personal Greetings, Admonition and Benediction	16:1-27

Author The author is Paul (1:1). Paul wrote Romans from Corinth on his third missionary journey. He was about to depart to Jerusalem (15:25-26). He left for Jerusalem from Philippi immediately after the Easter season (Acts 20:6). Since all the navigation on the Mediterranean Sea ceased after November 11 and was not resumed again until March 10, Romans was likely written before March 10. February 57 AD is probably an accurate date. One segment mentions Gentile (1:13; 11:13; 15:14, 16) and another Jews (2:17, 4:1 and ch. 16). There is some indication that the believers in Rome needed to be exhorted to live in harmony.

Recipient The recipient was the church in Rome (1:7).

Purpose The threefold purpose of Romans is educational, pastoral, and personal. The educational purpose is to teach that a sovereign God saves Jews and Gentiles by grace. Paul explains that God justifies, sanctifies, and glorifies. The pastoral purpose is to exhort Jewish and Gentile believers to live in harmony. Evidently, there was some tension between the Jews and the Gentiles in the church. (3:9, 29, 30; also *cf.* 3:1-2; 9:4-5 with 9-11 and 14-15). The personal purpose is to prepare for Paul's journey to Rome and beyond to Spain. Paul expects aid from them to carry the gospel to Spain (15:24).

Summary: The overall message is God is righteous to justify, sanctify, and glorify Jews and Gentiles by grace and to exhort both Jews and Gentiles to live harmoniously with each other.

The overall spiritual truth is God justifies by grace through faith, and believers should obey Him by living a loving life.

Romans 1:16 "For I am not ashamed of the gospel of Christ, for it is the power of God to salvation for everyone who believes, for the Jew first and also for the Greek."

Romans 2:11 "For there is no partiality with God."

Romans 3:23-26 "For all have sinned and fall short of the glory of God, being justified freely by His grace through the redemption that is in Christ Jesus, whom God set forth *as* a propitiation by His blood, through faith, to demonstrate His righteousness, because in His forbearance, God had passed over the sins that were previously committed to demonstrate at the present time His righteousness, that He might be just and the justifier of the one who has faith in Jesus."

Romans 5:8 "But God demonstrates His own love toward us, in that while we were still sinners, Christ died for us."

Romans 6:4 "Therefore, we were buried with Him through baptism into death, that just as Christ was raised from the dead by the glory of the Father, even so we also should walk in newness of life."

Romans 8:1 "T*here is* therefore now no condemnation to those who are in Christ Jesus, who do not walk according to the flesh, but according to the Spirit."

Romans 8:5 "For those who live according to the flesh set their minds on the things of the flesh, but those *who live* according to the Spirit, the things of the Spirit."

Romans 8:6 "For to be carnally minded *is* death, but to be spiritually minded *is* life and peace.

Romans 8:28 "And we know that all things work together for good to those who love God, to those who are the called according to *His* purpose."

Romans 12:1 "I beseech you therefore, brethren, by the mercies of God, that you present your bodies a living sacrifice, holy, acceptable to God, *which is* your reasonable service."

Romans 12:2 "And do not be conformed to this world, but be transformed by the renewing of your mind, that you may prove what *is* that good and acceptable and perfect will of God."

Romans 13:8-10 "Owe no one anything except to love one another, for he who loves another has fulfilled the law. For the commandments, 'You shall not commit adultery, You shall not murder, You shall not steal, You shall not bear false witness, You shall not covet,' and if *there is* any other commandment, are *all* summed up in this saying, namely, 'You shall love your neighbor as yourself. Love does no harm to a neighbor; therefore, love *is* the fulfillment of the law."

1 CORINTHIANS: DISORDERS IN THE CHURCH

Subject The subject of 1 Corinthians is disorders in the church.

Structure The overall structure is the format of an ancient letter. The body corresponds to the report from Chloe's household (1:11), the common report (5:1), and their letter (7:1).

I.	Salutation	1:1-3
II.	Thanksgiving	1:4-9
III.	The Body of the Letter	1:10-16-12
	A. Reaction to Chloe's Report (Division)	1:10-4:21
	B. Response to Common Report (Discipline)	5:1-6:20
	1. Incest	5:1-13
	2. Lawsuits	6:1-11
	3. Fornication	6:12-20
	C Reply to Corinthian Letter (Difficulties)	7:1-16:12
	1. Marriage	7:1-40
	2. Meats Offered to Idols	8:1-11:1
	3. Women's Head Coverings	11:2-16
	4. The Lord's Table	11:17-34
	5, Spiritual Gifts	12:1-14:40
	6. The Resurrection	15:1-58
	7. The Collection	16:1-4
	8. Travel Plans	16:5-12
IV.	Personal Greetings, Admonition and Benediction	16:13-24

Author Paul wrote 1 Corinthians (1:1; 16:21; also 1:12-17; 3:4; 6:22). On his second missionary journey, he established a church at Corinth (3:6; 4:15; Acts 18:1-17). He stayed for 18 months (51-52 AD). Later, he wrote 1 Corinthians from Ephesus (16:8). He was in Ephesus from 53 to 57 AD. Thus, he wrote 1 Corinthians in the early spring of 57 AD.

Recipient The recipient was the church in Corinth. While Paul was at Ephesus, he received reports concerning quarrels in the church of Corinth (1:11). The church sent a letter requesting Paul's opinion on several issues (7:1). From all this, it is evident that: 1) There were factions among the believers at Corinth. 2) There was gross immorality in the church, even incest. 3) They were taking each other to court. 4) Many practical matters troubled them.

Purposes The purposes are to correct the disorders and answer questions they submitted to him. The disorders in the church included divisions, incest, lawsuits, and fornication. They asked Paul questions about marriage, meats offered to idols, the veiling of women, the Lord's Table, spiritual gifts, the resurrection, and the collection for the poor saints in Jerusalem. He addresses these issues by instructing, rebuking, condemning, and commending them.

Summary: The overall message is believers should deal with problems according to the particular characteristics of each problem with the ultimate aim of living harmoniously in love.

The ultimate spiritual truth is to live according to truth and love.

1 Corinthians 1:9 "God *is* faithful, by whom you were called into the fellowship of His Son, Jesus Christ our Lord."

1 Corinthians 1:18 "For the message of the cross is foolishness to those who are perishing, but to us who are being saved it is the power of God."

1 Corinthians 2:14 "But the natural man does not receive the things of the Spirit of God, for they are foolishness to him; nor can he know *them,* because they are spiritually discerned."

1 Corinthians 6:20 "For you were bought at a price; therefore glorify God in your body and in your spirit, which are God's."

1 Corinthians 9:16 "For if I preach the gospel, I have nothing to boast of, for necessity is laid upon me; yes, woe is me if I do not preach the gospel!"

1 Corinthians 10:13 "No temptation has overtaken you except such as is common to man; but God *is* faithful, who will not allow you to be tempted beyond what you are able, but with the temptation will also make the way of escape, that you may be able to bear *it*."

1 Corinthians 10:23 "All things are lawful for me, but not all things are helpful; all things are lawful for me, but not all things edify."

1 Corinthians 10:31 "Therefore, whether you eat or drink, or whatever you do, do all to the glory of God."

1 Corinthians 13:2 "And though I have *the gift of* prophecy, and understand all mysteries and all knowledge, and though I have all faith, so that I could remove mountains, but have not love, I am nothing."

1 Corinthians 13:13 "And now abide faith, hope, love, these three; but the greatest of these *is* love."

1 Corinthians 15:1-4 "Moreover, brethren, I declare to you the gospel which I preached to you, which also you received and in which you stand, by which also you are saved if you hold fast that word which I preached to you—unless you believed in vain. For I delivered to you first of all that which I also received: that Christ died for our sins according to the Scriptures, and that He was buried, and that He rose again the third day according to the Scriptures."

1 Corinthians 15:33 "Do not be deceived: "Evil company corrupts good habits."

1 Corinthians 15:57 "But thanks *be* to God, who gives us the victory through our Lord Jesus Christ."

2 CORINTHIANS: THE TRUE MINISTRY

Subject The subject of 2 Corinthians is the true minister.
Structure The overall structure follows the format of an ancient letter.

I. Salutation	1:1-2
II. Thanksgiving	1:3-11
III. The Body of the Letter	1:12-13:10
A. Consolation (Comfort in the Ministry)	1:12-7:16
1. The Conduct of Paul	1:12-2:11
2. The Character of the Ministry	2:12-6:10
3. The Appeal to the Corinthians	6:11-7:16
B. Collection (The Ministry of Giving)	8:1-9:15
1. Arrangements for a Prepared Gift	8:1-9:5
2. Arguments for a Generous Gift	9:6-15
C. Vindication (Vindication of Paul's Ministry)	10:1-13:10
1. Readiness to Correct	10:1-12:18
2. Reluctance to Correct	12:19-13:10
IV. Personal Greetings, Admonition and Benediction	13:11-14

Author The author was Paul (1:1; 2:1). The events between the two epistles probably took place in seven or eight months. Thus, the date of 2 Corinthians is the fall of 57 AD.

Recipient The recipient was the church in Corinth. Paul most likely sent 1 Corinthians to Corinth with Titus. After he sent that letter, he became deeply concerned about how the Corinthians would receive it (7:8). He called them carnal (1 Cor. 3:1) and told them that some of them were proud (1 Cor. 4:18). So Paul left Ephesus and went to Troas, where he expected to meet Titus, but he did not find him there (2:12-13). Then, he departed for Macedonia (2:13), where he met Titus (7:6, 7), probably at Philippi. Titus informed him that the church supported him, but some highly critical of Paul were casting doubts in the minds of the Corinthians concerning his integrity.

These opponents of Paul accused him of walking according to the flesh (1:12, 17; 10:2), being deceitful (2:17; 4:2; 12:16), intimidating people with his letters (10:9-10), unjustly mistreating someone to the point of ruining him (7:2), and defrauding people (7:2). More specifically, he had promised to return and didn't (1:15-17, 23; 2:1-4), mishandled the discipline of the incestuous fellow (7:2; 10:8; 13:7-10; also 2:5-11) and he didn't take money on his first trip, but was planning on "fleecing the flock" under the guise of a collection for the poor saints of Jerusalem on his next trip (8:20). This situation produced a number of problems. First and foremost, these accusations raised questions in the minds of the Corinthians. They began to withdraw from Paul, at least emotionally. Also, would he be discouraged? Furthermore, he needed to address the situation concerning those falsely accusing him.

Purpose The major purpose is to defend and vindicate his apostolic authority. Paul's opponents had made a threefold assault on him. They attacked his person (10:10, 11:6), his character (1:11-17; 12:16-19), and his teaching (2:17; 11:4). He was accused of fickleness (1:17,

18, 23), of pride and boasting (3:1; 5:12), of obscurity in preaching (4:3), of weakness (10:10), of rudeness of speech (11:6), of being contemptible in person (4:7-10; 6:4-10; 10:10; 12:7-10), of being dishonest (12:16-19), of being hardly sound of mind (5:13; 11:16-19; 12:6), and of not being an apostle (11:5; 12:12). Paul answers each of these charges on his person (10:7; 13:4) and on his character (4:1 2; 1:15-24; 12:14-18; 7:2; 5:13). There are several minor purposes, including 1) giving needed instruction regarding the penitent offender (2:5-11), probably the man mentioned in 1 Corinthians 5, 2, furnishing further instruction regarding the offering for the poor saints in Jerusalem (2 Cor. 9:1-5), and 3) showing his care for them (7:12).

Summary: The overall message is to express Paul's care and concern for them, to give them some further instruction about the collection for the poor, and to vindicate his authority.

The overall spiritual truth is the true minister cares about people, is comforted in ministry, and sometimes must defend himself.

2 Corinthians 1:8-9 "For we do not want you to be ignorant, brethren, of our trouble which came to us in Asia: that we were burdened beyond measure, above strength, so that we despaired even of life. Yes, we had the sentence of death in ourselves, that we should not trust in ourselves but in God who raises the dead.

2 Corinthians 3:18 "But we all, with unveiled face, beholding as in a mirror the glory of the Lord, are being transformed into the same image from glory to glory, just as by the Spirit of the Lord."

2 Corinthians 4:8-10 "We are hard-pressed on every side, yet not crushed; *we are* perplexed, but not in despair; persecuted, but not forsaken; struck down, but not destroyed—always carrying about in the body the dying of the Lord Jesus, that the life of Jesus also may be manifested in our body."

2 Corinthians 5:7 "For we walk by faith, not by sight."

2 Corinthians 5:8 "We are confident, yes, well pleased rather to be absent from the body and to be present with the Lord."

2 Corinthians 5:17 "Therefore, if anyone *is* in Christ, *he is* a new creation; old things have passed away; behold, all things have become new."

2 Corinthians 5:21 "For He made Him who knew no sin *to be* sin for us, that we might become the righteousness of God in Him."

2 Corinthians 7:10 "For godly sorrow produces repentance *leading* to salvation, not to be regretted; but the sorrow of the world produces death."

2 Corinthians 9:6 "But this *I say:* He who sows sparingly will also reap sparingly, and he who sows bountifully will also reap bountifully."

2 Corinthians 9:8 "And God *is* able to make all grace abound toward you, that you, always having all sufficiency in all *things,* may have an abundance for every good work."

2 Corinthians 12:7 "And lest I should be exalted above measure by the abundance of the revelations, a thorn in the flesh was given to me, a messenger of Satan to buffet me, lest I be exalted above measure."

2 Corinthians 12:9-10 "And He said to me, 'My grace is sufficient for you, for My strength is made perfect in weakness.' Therefore most gladly, I will rather boast in my infirmities that the power of Christ may rest upon me. Therefore, I take pleasure in infirmities, in reproaches, in needs, in persecutions, in distresses, for Christ's sake. For when I am weak, then I am strong."

GALATIANS: FREEDOM FROM THE MOSAIC LAW

Subject The subject is liberty, freedom from the Mosaic Law.

Structure Galatians is in the form of an ancient letter with one exception. Paul omitted the thanksgiving. By so doing, he is subtly saying, "I'm not thankful for those who move away from the Gospel." By the way, he thanked God for the Corinthians.

I. Salutation	1:1-5
II. Situation	1:6-10
III. The Body of the Letter	1:11-6:10
A. Personal (Paul got his Gospel from God)	1:11-2:21
1. Origin of the Gospel	1:11-24
2. Confirmation of the Gospel	2:1-10
3. Content of the Gospel	2:11-21
B. Doctrinal (the Gospel sets the believer free from the law)	3:1-4:31
1. Proven from the Experience of the Galatians	3:1-5
2. Proven from the Example of Abraham	3:6-9
3. Proven from the Nature of the Law	3:10-14
4. Proven from the Priority of the Promise	3:15-18
5. Proven from the Purpose of the Law	3:19-29
6. Proven from the Adoption of Sons	4:1-11
7. Personal Appeal	4:12-20
8. An Allegory	4:21-31
C. Practical (Stand in liberty and love)	5:1-6:10
1. Stand in Freedom	5:1-12
2. Love by Walking in the Spirit	5:13-26
3. Restore Fallen Brethren	6:1-5
4. Give and Do Good Works	6:6-10
IV. Personal Greetings, Admonition, and Benediction	6:11-18

Author The author was Paul (1:1; 5:2). Paul wrote in 49 AD before the Jerusalem Council.

Recipients The recipients were the churches in the province of Galatia. On the first missionary journey (Acts 13:13-14:23), Paul and Barnabas started churches in Galatia (modern Turkey). Paul visited them twice (4:13). Shortly after his last visit (1:6), Judaizers said Paul perverted apostolic teaching and taught the Galatians must keep the Law, including the observance of days (4:10) and circumcision (5:1-12; 6:11-15). They started keeping the law (4:9-10) and were about to be circumcised (5:2; 6:12

Purpose The purposes are refuting Judaizers and keeping Galatians from getting circumcised.

Summary: The overall message is since the gospel of the grace of God, justification by faith, is from God, believers should stand in the freedom from the Law, not be circumcised, and use their freedom to live a life of love.

The overall spiritual truth is that since believers are not under Mosaic law, they should live by faith in dependence upon the Holy Spirit to live a life of love.

Galatians 2:20 "I have been crucified with Christ; it is no longer I who live, but Christ lives in me; and the *life* which I now live in the flesh I live by faith in the Son of God, who loved me and gave Himself for me."

Galatians 5:1 "Stand fast therefore in the liberty by which Christ has made us free, and do not be entangled again with a yoke of bondage."

Galatians 5:13 "For you, brethren, have been called to liberty; only do not *use* liberty as an opportunity for the flesh, but through love serve one another."

Galatians 5:14 "For all the law is fulfilled in one word, *even* in this: 'You shall love your neighbor as yourself.'"

Galatians 5:16 "I say then: Walk in the Spirit, and you shall not fulfill the lust of the flesh."

Galatians 5:19-21 "Now the works of the flesh are evident, which are: adultery, fornication, uncleanness, lewdness, idolatry, sorcery, hatred, contentions, jealousies, outbursts of wrath, selfish ambitions, dissensions, heresies, envy, murders, drunkenness, revelries, and the like; of which I tell you beforehand, just as I also told *you* in time past, that those who practice such things will not inherit the kingdom of God."

Galatians 5:22-23 "But the fruit of the Spirit is love, joy, peace, longsuffering, kindness, goodness, faithfulness, gentleness, self-control. Against such, there is no law."

After his first journey, Paul wrote *one* epistle: Galatians.

On his second journey, Paul wrote *two* epistles: 1 and 2 Thessalonians.

On his third missionary journey, Paul wrote *three* epistles: Romans, 1 Corinthians, and 2 Corinthians.

On his fourth trip, Paul wrote *four* epistles: Ephesians, Philippians, Colossians and Philemon. These are called prison epistles because he wrote them while in prison in Rome.

On his fifth trip, Paul wrote 1 and 2 Timothy and Titus.

EPHESIANS: THE CALLING OF THE BELIEVER

Subject The subject of Ephesians is the believer's calling (1:18; 4:1).

Structure Ephesians is in the format of an ancient letter, but here, that is tricky. Paul begins with a thanksgiving and a prayer (1:3-23). In the midst of the prayer, he develops several other themes. Then, he continued the prayer (3:1) but again wandered off on another subject. Finally, he comes back and finishes the prayer (3:14). The body of the epistle is divided into two parts: calling and conduct.

I. Salutation	1:1-2
II. Thanksgiving	1:3-14
III. Prayer	1:15-23
IV The Body of the Letter	2:1-6:20
A. The Calling of the Church	2:1-3:21
1. Our Calling Individually (Regeneration)	2:1-10
2. Our Calling Corporately (Reconciliation)	2:11-22
3. The Revelation of this Calling (Revelation)	3:1-13
4. Prayer for Power and Perception	3:14-21
B. The Conduct of the Church	4:1-6:20
1. Walk in Unity (in church)	4:1-16
2. Walk in Righteousness (in the Flesh)	4:17-32
3. Walk in Love	5:1-7
4. Walk in the Light (in the World)	5:8-14
5. Walk in Wisdom	5:15-21
6. Walk in Submission (at home)	5:22-6:9
7. Walk in Strength, Stand in the Armor of God (Warfare)	6:10-20
V. Greeting and benediction	6:21-14

Author Paul was the author (1:1; 3:1). He was in prison at the time (4:1), that is, his two-year imprisonment in Rome (Acts 28:30-31). The date was 61 AD. Ephesians was written to the church at Ephesus and to all believers everywhere (1:1).

Recipient The recipient was the church in Ephesus.

Purpose The major purpose of Ephesians is to enlighten believers concerning their calling so they would walk worthy of it. A minor purpose is to encourage the recipients not to lose heart (3:13). Paul's imprisonment discouraged many believers. Thus, he says, don't feel sorry for me or be discouraged by what has happened. God has especially blessed me in revealing to me the mystery of the church.

Summary: The overall message is since believers are called to be in Christ in the church, they should live a worthy life in unity, righteousness, love, and wisdom, stand against all the forces that would move them away from that lifestyle, and not lose heart.

The overall spiritual truth is since believers are called to be in Christ in the church, they should walk worthy of their calling.

Ephesians 1:3 "Blessed be the God and Father of our Lord Jesus Christ, who has blessed us with every spiritual blessing in the heavenly places in Christ."

Ephesians 2:8-10 "For by grace you have been saved through faith, and that not of yourselves; it is the gift of God, not of works, lest anyone should boast. For we are His workmanship, created in Christ Jesus for good works, which God prepared beforehand that we should walk in them."

Ephesians 3:6 [The mystery is] "that the Gentiles should be fellow heirs, of the same body, and partakers of His promise in Christ through the gospel."

Ephesians 3:16 "that He would grant you, according to the riches of His glory, to be strengthened with might through His Spirit in the inner man."

Ephesians 4:1 "I, therefore, the prisoner of the Lord, beseech you to walk worthy of the calling with which you were called."

Ephesians 4:30-32 "And do not grieve the Holy Spirit of God, by whom you were sealed for the day of redemption. Let all bitterness, wrath, anger, clamor, and evil speaking be put away from you, with all malice. And be kind to one another, tenderhearted, forgiving one another, even as God in Christ forgave you."

Ephesians 5:18 "And do not be drunk with wine, in which is dissipation; but be filled with the Spirit."

Ephesians 6:13 "Therefore take up the whole armor of God, that you may be able to withstand in the evil day, and having done all, to stand."

Paul wrote four epistles while in prison in Rome: Ephesians, Philippians, Colossians, and Philemon. In all four, he mentions his chains (Eph. 3:1; Phil. 4:14; Col. 4:10; Philem. 9). Of the four, Colossians was probably written first. Paul wrote it because of the need. Then, after reflection, he penned Ephesians. It seems evident that Colossians and Ephesians were written before Philippians or at least that Philippians was written last.

PHILIPPIANS: LIVING WORTHY OF THE GOSPEL

Subject The subject of Philippians is living worthy of the gospel.
Structure It is in the format of an ancient letter.

I. Salutation	1:1-2
II. Thanksgiving	1:3-8
III. Prayer	1:9-11
IV. The Body of the Letter	1:12-4:21
A. Paul's Situation (prison resulted in the spread of the gospel)	1:12-26
B. Philippians' Situation (live worthy of the Gospel)	1:27-4:9
1. Live Worthy of the Gospel	1:27-30
2. Be Unified by Having a Humble Concern for Others	2:1-30
3. Stand Fast in the Lord	3:1-4:1
4. Live in Peace	4:2-9
C. Paul's Response (To their Support of his Gospel Ministry)	4:10-20
V. Greetings and Benediction	4:21-23

Author Philippians 1:1 identifies the authors as Paul and Timothy, but evidently, Paul alone was the author. He immediately, and throughout the letter, speaks in the first person. When he does mention Timothy in chapter 2, it is in the third person. Paul was in prison when he wrote (see "my chains" in 1:7, 13, 14). Furthermore, he was in prison in Rome, for he refers to the whole Praetorian Guard (1:13) and Caesar's household (4:22). So, Philippians was written from Rome to the church at Philippi in 62 AD.

Recipient The recipient was the church in Philippi. They were concerned about Paul (1:12) and had sent Epaphroditus to Rome with financial support (2:25; 1:5; 4:10, 14-16). They evidently had a small problem with unity (1:27; 2:2; 3:16; 4:2-3, 9) and they were at least feeling some pressure from the Judaizers (3:1-16). They were concerned about Paul; Paul was concerned about them (2:19, 24).

Purpose The immediate purpose was to thank them for their financial support. The Philippian church had sent Epaphroditus with money to Rome for Paul (2:25-30, esp. 2:25, 30). Paul thanked them for their gift (1:5; 4:10-20). He also wrote to explain his situation (1:12-26 and 2:24) and exhort them to live worthy of the gospel by being unified, having a humble concern for others, standing fast in the Lord, and living in peace.

Summary: The overall message is that Paul thanked them for their financial support, informed them that the Lord was using him to spread the gospel, and urged them to live worthy of it.

The overall spiritual truth is believers should live worthy of the gospel by standing fast in it and striving together for it.

Philippians 1:21 "For to me, to live *is* Christ, and to die *is* gain."

Philippians 1:23 "For I am hard-pressed between the two, having a desire to depart and be with Christ, *which is* far better."

Philippians 2:5 "Let this mind be in you which was also in Christ Jesus."

Philippians 3:8-10 "Yet indeed I also count all things loss for the excellence of the knowledge of Christ Jesus my Lord, for whom I have suffered the loss of all things, and count them as rubbish, that I may gain Christ and be found in Him, not having my own righteousness, which *is* from the law, but that which *is* through faith in Christ, the righteousness which is from God by faith; that I may know Him and the power of His resurrection, and the fellowship of His sufferings, being conformed to His death,

Philippians 3:20 "For our citizenship is in heaven, from which we also eagerly wait for the Savior, the Lord Jesus Christ."

Philippians 4:5 "Let your gentleness be known to all men. The Lord *is* at hand."

Philippians 4:6-7 "Be anxious for nothing, but in everything by prayer and supplication, with thanksgiving, let your requests be made known to God and the peace of God, which surpasses all understanding, will guard your hearts and minds through Christ Jesus."

Philippians 4:8 "Finally, brethren, whatever things are true, whatever things *are* noble, whatever things *are* just, whatever things *are* pure, whatever things *are* lovely, whatever things *are* of good report, if *there is* any virtue and if *there is* anything praiseworthy—meditate on these things."

Philippians 4:13 "I can do all things through Christ who strengthens me."

Philippians 4:19 "And my God shall supply all your need according to His riches in glory by Christ Jesus."

COLOSSIANS: THE SUFFICIENCY OF CHRIST

Subject The subject is the sufficiency of Christ for the spiritual life.
Structure Colossians is a perfect example of the pattern of an ancient letter.

I. Salutation	1:1-2
II. Thanksgiving	1:3-8
III. Prayer	1:9-14
IV The Body of the Letter	1:15-4:6
A. Doctrinal: Sufficiency of Christ Declared	1:15-2:7
1. Christ Suffered to Bring Believers to Maturity	1:15-23
2 Paul Also Suffered to Bring Believers to Maturity	1:24-29
3. Paul Exhorted Believers to Grow toward Maturity	2:1-7
B. Defense: Sufficiency of Christ Defended	2:8-3:4
1. Stated Positively	2:8-15
2. Stated Negatively	2:16-3:4
C. Duty: Sufficiency of Christ Displayed	3:5-4:6
1. In Personal Life	3:5-14
2 In Church Life	3:15-17
3 In Home Life	3:18-21
4. In Business Life	3:22-4:1
5 In Social Life	4:2-6
V. Greetings and Benediction	4:7-18

Author Paul, along with Timothy, wrote Colossians (1:1). Colossians was written from Rome by Paul in 61 AD.

Recipient Paul addresses the epistle to "the saints and faithful brethren in Christ, which are at Colosse" (1:2). A heresy threatened the church at Colosse. So Epaphras journeyed to Rome to report to Paul on the conditions at Colosse. His visit prompted the letter. The believers at Colosse were saved, sound, and growing (1:3-8; 2:5). The heresy that threatened to sidetrack them was a mixture of Jewish legalism (2:16-17), mysticism (2:18-19), and asceticism (2:20-22).

Purpose Paul's primary purpose was to warn them about Judaistic, mystical asceticism (2:16-3:4), which was a mixture of Jewish legalism, Greek philosophical speculation, and Gentile asceticism (2:4, 8, 16, 18, 20). Christ is sufficient. Believers do not need rules, revelations, and regulations. The second purpose was to encourage believers to give Christ preeminence in everything. Paul's purpose is like a coin—it has two sides. One is positive and the other is negative. The negative side is to refute the false teaching. The positive side is to encourage believers to grow, to go on to maturity, and to give Christ preeminence in everything (2:5-7).

Summary: The overall message is that since Christ is the supreme sovereign and sufficient Savior, believers should beware of any teaching that suggests they need something other than Jesus Christ, and they should see to it that Jesus Christ has the preeminence in everything.

The overall spiritual truth is the sufficiency of Christ for the spiritual life.

Colossians 1:9-12 "For this reason we also, since the day we heard it, do not cease to pray for you, and to ask that you may be filled with the knowledge of His will in all wisdom and spiritual understanding; that you may walk worthy of the Lord, fully pleasing *Him,* being fruitful in every good work and increasing in the knowledge of God; strengthened with all might, according to His glorious power, for all patience and longsuffering with joy; giving thanks to the Father who has qualified us to be partakers of the inheritance of the saints in the light."

Colossians 2:8-10 "Beware lest anyone cheat you through philosophy and empty deceit, according to the tradition of men, according to the basic principles of the world, and not according to Christ. For in Him dwells all the fullness of the Godhead bodily; and you are complete in Him, who is the head of all principality and power."

<u>**Colossians 3:14-17**</u> "But above all these things put on love, which is the bond of perfection. And let the peace of God rule in your hearts, to which also you were called in one body; and be thankful. Let the word of Christ dwell in you richly in all wisdom, teaching and admonishing one another in psalms and hymns and spiritual songs, singing with grace in your hearts to the Lord. And *whatever* you do in word or deed, *do* all in the name of the Lord Jesus, giving thanks to God the Father through Him."

<u>**Colossians 4:5-6**</u> "Walk in wisdom toward those *who are* outside, redeeming the time. Let your speech always *be* with grace, seasoned with salt, that you may know how you ought to answer each one."

1 THESSALONIANS: THE BOOK OF SANCTIFICATION

Subject The subject of 1 Thessalonians is sanctification (5:23).

Structure First Thessalonians is a letter. It begins with a salutation (1:1) and a thanksgiving (1:2-12). A prayer would be expected next, but Paul defends his ministry instead. Then, he returns to thanksgiving (2:13-16), after which he returns to a discussion of his relationship to them (2:17-3:10). Finally, he prays (3:11-13). In Ephesians, he interrupted his prayer. Here, he interrupted his thanksgiving.

I Salutation	1:1
II. Thanksgiving	1:2-10
III. The Body of the Letter	2:1-5:24
A. Personal (their Faith)	2:1-3:13
1. Paul's Past Character among Them	2:1-12
2. Paul's Thankfulness for Them	2:13-16
3. Paul's Present concern for Them	2:17-3:10
4. Paul's Prayer for Them	3:11-13
B. Practical (their Love)	4:1-12
1. General Exhortation	4:1, 2
2. Specific Applications	4:3-12
C. Prophetical (their Hope)	4:13-5:11
1. The Rapture	4:13-18
2. The Day of the Lord	5:1-11
D. Polity	5:12-24
1. Esteem the Elders	5:12, 13
2. Minister to Members	5:14, 15
3. Walk in God's Will	5:16-18
4. Discern True Doctrine	5:19-22
5. Prayer	5:23, 24
IV. Personal Greeting and Benediction	5:25-28

Author First Thessalonians 1:1 says the authors were Paul, Silas, and Timothy. "We" is used of the authors (1:2; 2:13; 2:17; 3:11; 4:1; 5:12), but the main author is Paul (1:1; 2:18; see "I" in 3:5; 4:13; 5:27). Paul then wrote 1 Thessalonians from Corinth in 51 AD.

Recipient The recipient was the church in Thessalonica. After Paul and Silas established a church in Thessalonica, they left when persecution broke out. Paul desired to return (2:18; 3:10), but since that was not possible, he sent Timothy (3:1-12), who brought back a good report (3:6).

Purpose The purpose was to encourage them in their faith, to exhort them to grow, establish them in hope, and enlighten them in church matters.

Summary: The overall message is believers are to be more and more set apart unto the Lord in their personal and assembly life.

The overall spiritual truth is sanctification consists of faith, love, and hope in one's personal life and church life. Sanctification is growing to maturity in faith, love, and hope.

1 Thessalonians 1:9-10 "For they themselves declare concerning us what manner of entry we had to you, and how you turned to God from idols to serve the living and true God, and to wait for His Son from heaven, whom He raised from the dead, *even* Jesus who delivers us from the wrath to come."

1 Thessalonians 2:1-2 "For you yourselves know, brethren, that our coming to you was not in vain. But even after we had suffered before and were spitefully treated at Philippi, as you know, we were bold in our God to speak to you the gospel of God in much conflict."

1 Thessalonians 4:3 "For this is the will of God, your sanctification: that you should abstain from sexual immorality."

1 Thessalonians 4:13-18 "But I do not want you to be ignorant, brethren, concerning those who have fallen asleep, lest you sorrow as others who have no hope. For if we believe that Jesus died and rose again, even so God will bring with Him those who sleep in Jesus. For this we say to you by the word of the Lord, that we who are alive *and* remain until the coming of the Lord will by no means precede those who are asleep. For the Lord Himself will descend from heaven with a shout, with the voice of an archangel, and with the trumpet of God. And the dead in Christ will rise first. Then we who are alive *and* remain shall be caught up together with them in the clouds to meet the Lord in the air. And thus, we shall always be with the Lord. Therefore comfort one another with these words."

1 Thessalonians 5:9 "For God did not appoint us to wrath, but to obtain salvation through our Lord Jesus Christ."

1 Thessalonians 5:16 "Rejoice always."
1 Thessalonians 5:17 "Pray without ceasing."
1 Thessalonians 5:18 "In everything give thanks; for this is the will of God in Christ Jesus for you."
1 Thessalonians 5:22 "Abstain from every form of evil."
1 Thessalonians 5:23 "Now may the God of peace Himself sanctify you completely; and may your whole spirit, soul, and body be preserved blameless at the coming of our Lord Jesus Christ."

2 THESSALONIANS: CORRECTION OF PROPHECY

Subject The subject of 2 Thessalonians is a correction of a prophetical misunderstanding.
Structure Second Thessalonians is in the form of an ancient letter.

I. Salutation	1:1-2
II. Thanksgiving	1:3-10
III. Prayer	1:11-12
IV. The Body of the Letter	2:1-3:16
A. Instructor: The Day of Christ has not Come	2:1-17
1. Instruction (Do Not Be Soon Shaken)	2:1-12
2. Thanksgiving (Stand Fast and Hold to the Word)	2:13-15
3. Prayer	2:16-17
B. Injunctions: Pray and Withdraw from the Disorderly	3:1-16
1. Call to Prayer	3:1-5
2. Command to Discipline	3:6-15
3. Concluding Prayer	3:16
V. Personal Greeting and Benediction	3:17-18

Author Second Thessalonians 1:1 says the epistle was written by Paul, Silas, and Timothy. "We" and "us" is used (1:3; 2:1; 2:13; 3:1, 3:4, 3:6, 3:14; etc.). The letter ends with Paul speaking in the first person singular (3:17). Paul is "the" author and Silas and Timothy are "linked together" with him. Paul wrote 2 Thessalonians a short time after 1 Thessalonians, which means he wrote it from Corinth in 51 AD.

Recipient The recipient was the church in Thessalonica. They concluded that the Day of the Christ had already arrived (2:2) and thus were expecting the immediate return of Christ. Consequently, some quit working. With leisure time on their hands, some became busybodies, interfering with those who wanted to work (3:10-12).

Purpose The purpose was to comfort them in their persecution, to correct a prophetical misunderstanding, and to commend them in their practice. Paul also issues several commands: to pray (3:1-5) and to withdraw from those who walk disorderly (3:6-15). This second command is related to the misconception of prophecy. Because they were expecting the Lord to come at any moment, some quit their jobs and became busybodies. Paul says that if people do not work, neither shall they eat (3:10), and you should withdraw yourself from them (3:6).

Summary: The overall message is believers should be comforted in the persecution, correct in their understanding of prophecy, not cease to work, and they should discipline those who do stop working.

The overall spiritual truth is the Lord is coming back and believers should work until He comes.

2 Thessalonians 2:1 "Now, brethren, concerning the coming of our Lord Jesus Christ and our gathering together to Him, we ask you, not to be soon shaken in mind or troubled, either by spirit or by word or by letter, as if from us, as though the day of Christ had come."

2 Thessalonians 2:13 "But we are bound to give thanks to God always for you, brethren beloved by the Lord, because God from the beginning chose you for salvation through sanctification by the Spirit and belief in the truth."

2 Thessalonians 3:1-2 "Finally, brethren, pray for us, that the word of the Lord may run swiftly and be glorified, just as it is with you, and that we may be delivered from unreasonable and wicked men; for not all have faith."

2 Thessalonians 3:10 "For even when we were with you, we commanded you this: If anyone will not work, neither shall he eat."

2 Thessalonians 3:14-15 "And if anyone does not obey our word in this epistle, note that person and do not keep company with him, that he may be ashamed. Yet do not count him as an enemy, but admonish him as a brother."

1 TIMOTHY: CONDUCT IN THE CHURCH

Subject The subject is the conduct at church (1:4, 1:18; 3:14-15; 6:20; also, 4:11; 6:2b).

Structure First Timothy is a letter, but there is no prayer and the thanksgiving is for what God has done for the author, not for the recipients.

I.	Salutation	1:1-2
II.	Introduction (Paul's charge, esp. 1:18)	1:3-20
III.	The Body of the Letter	2:1-6:21a
	A. The Charge Concerning Church Meetings	2:1-15
	1. Concerning Men	2:1-8
	2. Concerning Women	2:9-15
	B. The Charge Concerning Church Officers	3:1-13
	1. Concerning Elders	3:1-7
	2. Concerning Deacons	3:8-13
	C. The Charge Concerning Church Doctrine	3:14-4:16
	1. Concerning True Teaching	3:14-16
	2. Concerning False Teaching	4:1-11
	3. Concerning the Teacher	4:12-16
	D. The Charge Concerning Church Members	5:1-6:19
	1. Concerning the Old and the Young	5:1, 2
	2. Concerning Widows	5:3-16
	3. Concerning Elders	5:17-25
	4. Concerning Slaves	6:1, 2
	5. Concerning False Teachers	6:3-16
	6. Concerning the Rich	6:17-19
	E. Conclusion	6:20-21a
IV.	Benediction	6:21b

Author Paul was the author (1:1). Paul possibly wrote from Philippi in 62 AD.

Recipients The recipients were Timothy and the church at Ephesus (see plural "you" in 6:20). After Paul was released from prison in Rome and returned to Ephesus, he found erroneous teaching. He dealt with the leaders (1:18, 19) but anticipated further difficulty (1:3). So when he left, he put Timothy in charge (1:3). Once in Macedonia, he saw he was going to be delayed.

Purpose The purpose was to tell Timothy and the church at Ephesus how they were to conduct themselves in the church (3:15).

Summary: The overall message is proper conduct in the house of God (church), including the meetings, officers, teaching, and members.

The overall spiritual truth is church leaders are to refute error and teach truth, which leads to godliness.

The truth, in this case, is the doctrine spelled out in 1 Timothy 3:16, which leads to faith, a pure life and a good conscience, and godliness and love (1:3-5).

1 Timothy 1:16 "However, for this reason I obtained mercy, that in me first Jesus Christ might show all longsuffering, as a pattern to those who are going to believe on Him for everlasting life."

1 Timothy 2:12 "And" I do not permit a woman to teach or to have authority over a man, but to be in silence."

1 Timothy 3:15-16 "but if I am delayed, *I write* so that you may know how you ought to conduct yourself in the house of God, which is the church of the living God, the pillar and ground of the truth. And without controversy great is the mystery of godliness: God was manifested in the flesh, Justified in the Spirit, Seen by angels, Preached among the Gentiles, Believed on in the world, Received up in glory."

1 Timothy 4:8 "For bodily exercise profits a little, but godliness is profitable for all things, having promise of the life that now is and of that which is to come."

1 Timothy 4:12 "Let no one despise your youth, but be an example to the believers in word, in conduct, in love, in spirit, in faith, in purity."

1 Timothy 6:10 "For the love of money is a root of all *kinds of* evil, for which some have strayed from the faith in their greediness, and pierced themselves through with many sorrows."

1 Timothy 6:17-19 "Command those who are rich in this present age not to be haughty, nor to trust in uncertain riches but in the living God, who gives us richly all things to enjoy. Let them do good, that they be rich in good works, ready to give, willing to share, storing up for themselves a good foundation for the time to come, that they may lay hold on eternal life."

2 TIMOTHY: THE MINISTRY OF THE WORD

Subject The subject 2 Timothy is fulfill your ministry or be faithful to the ministry that God has given you (4.5b and 1.6).

Structure Second Timothy is in the form of an ancient letter with one exception. It does not have the prayer, which usually follows the thanksgiving. The body is a series of commands.

I. Salutation	1:1-2
II. Thanksgiving	1:3-5
III. Prologue	1:6-18
IV. The Body of the Letter	2:1-4:10
A. Commit the Word to Faithful Teachers	2:1-13
1. Be Strong	2:1
2. Commit the Word	2:2
3. Endure Hardness	2:3-13
B. Correct Errorists	2:14-26
1. Charge Them	2:14, 15
2. Avoid Empty Disputes	2:16-21
3. Pursue Righteousness	2:22-26
C. Continue in the Word	3:1-4:8
1. In Personal Life	3:1-17
2. In Public Ministry	4:1-8
V. Epilogue	4:9-10
VI. Personal Greetings and Benediction	4:19-22

Author The author was Paul (1:1). Nero, emperor of Rome from AD 54 to 68, was responsible for the beginning of the Roman persecution of Christians. When Paul returned from Spain in 66 AD, he was regarded "as a criminal" (2:9), arrested, and put in a cold Roman cell (4:13) without hope of acquittal (4:6-8, 17, 18). Under these conditions, Paul wrote 2 Timothy in the fall of 67 AD, hoping that Timothy would be able to visit him before winter (4:21).

Recipient The recipient was Timothy. In 2 Timothy, Timothy is still in Ephesus. Some of that old problem is left (2:14-18), but the issue is not so much that as the dark days. For one thing, Paul was facing martyrdom, but beyond that, they were perilous days indeed.

Purpose The purpose was to strengthen Timothy and summon him to Rome as soon as possible (1:4; 4:1, 21a). Perhaps Paul also needed Mark for ministry (4:11), as well as his cloak, books, and parchments, which he left in Troas (4:13).

Summary: The overall message is Timothy is encourage to fulfill his ministry in spite of persecution and defection and to summon him to come to Rome.

The overall spiritual truths is in dark, difficult days, when there is persecution from without (1:8, and maybe 3:1-9; 4:14), and defection from within (1:15; 2:14, 2:16-18, 2:25) make sure to fulfill your ministry.

2 Timothy 2:2 "And the things that you have heard from me among many witnesses, commit these to faithful men who will be able to teach others also."

2 Timothy 2:11-13 "This is a faithful saying: For if we died with *Him,* We shall also live with *Him.* If we endure, We shall also reign with *Him.* If we deny *Him,* He also will deny us. If we are faithless, He remains faithful; He cannot deny Himself."

2 Timothy 2:22 "Flee also youthful lusts; but pursue righteousness, faith, love, peace with those who call on the Lord out of a pure heart."

2 Timothy 2:23-26 "But avoid foolish and ignorant disputes, knowing that they generate strife. And a servant of the Lord must not quarrel but be gentle to all, able to teach, patient, in humility correcting those who are in opposition, if God perhaps will grant them repentance, so that they may know the truth, and *that* they may come to their senses *and escape* the snare of the devil, having been taken captive by him to *do* his will."

2 Timothy 3:16-17 "All Scripture *is* given by inspiration of God, and *is* profitable for doctrine, for reproof, for correction, for instruction in righteousness, that the man of God may be complete, thoroughly equipped for every good work.

2 Timothy 4:1-2 "I charge *you* therefore before God and the Lord Jesus Christ, who will judge the living and the dead at His appearing and His kingdom: Preach the word! Be ready in season *and* out of season. Convince, rebuke, exhort, with all longsuffering and teaching."

TITUS: ORDER IN THE CHURCH

Subject The subject of Titus is church order.

Structure Titus follows the form of an ancient letter, except there is no thanksgiving or prayer. In the body of the book, Paul gives three commands, each followed by a reason for it (see 1:5 and *for* in 1:10; 2:1 and *for* in 2:11; 3:1 and *for* in 3:3).

I. Salutation	1:1-4
II. The Body of the Letter	1:5-3:11
A. Ordain Elders	1:5-16
1. Qualifications for Elders	1:5-9
2. Reasons for Elders	1:10-12
3. Response to Errorists	1:13-16
B. Speak about Godliness	2:1-15
1. To the Older	2:2-5
2. To the Younger	2:6
3. To Yourself	2:7-8
4. To Slaves	2:9-10
5. Reason for Speaking	2:11-15
C. Remind about Good Works	3:1-7
1. Tell all to do Good Works	3:1, 2
2. Reason for Reminder	3:3-7
D. Conclusion	3:8-11
III. Personal Greetings and Benediction	3:12-15

Author The author was Paul (1:1). After Acts 28, Paul went to Ephesus and Macedonia (probably Philippi). Then, he journeyed to Crete, where he left Titus (1:5). Then he traveled to Corinth, where he wrote Titus. From there, he went to Spain and on a return trip, he was arrested. The date is 62 AD.

Recipient The recipient was Titus. The churches on the island of Crete needed organization (1:5). Jewish teachers needed to be rebuked (1:10, 13). They were going to the genealogies of the Old Testament (3:9) and constructing the fables (1:14). From these myths, they drew commandments that turned people from the truth of God to the commandments of men. Furthermore, their motives were wrong and the results were not God-honoring. Their motive was money (1:11). Their "ministry" produced disputes, contentions, and strivings about the law (3:9), as well as subverting whole households. They needed instruction in godliness and good works.

Purpose The purpose was to instruct Titus, impart personal information to Titus concerning Zenas and Apollos (3:13), and to inform Titus of Paul's decision to spend the winter at Nicopolis (3:12). The letter notified Titus that Paul was planning to send either Artemas or Tychicus to replace him and that he wished for Titus to join him at Nicopolis.

Summary: The overall message is to set things in order in the churches.

The overall spiritual truth is to put things in order by ordaining elders, who are to see that the Word is taught, producing godliness and good works.

Titus 1:5 "For this reason, I left you in Crete, that you should set in order the things that are lacking, and appoint elders in every city as I commanded you."

Titus 2:11-14 "For the grace of God that brings salvation has appeared to all men, teaching us that, denying ungodliness and worldly lusts, we should live soberly, righteously, and godly in the present age, looking for the blessed hope and glorious appearing of our great God and Savior Jesus Christ, who gave Himself for us, that He might redeem us from every lawless deed and purify for Himself *His* own special people, zealous for good works.

Titus 3:4-5 "But when the kindness and the love of God our Savior toward man appeared, not by works of righteousness which we have done, but according to His mercy He saved us, through the washing of regeneration and renewing of the Holy Spirit."

Titus 3:8-9 "This is a faithful saying, and these things I want you to affirm constantly, that those who have believed in God should be careful to maintain good works. These things are good and profitable to men. But avoid foolish disputes, genealogies, contentions, and strivings about the law; for they are unprofitable and useless."

PHILEMON: AN EXAMPLE OF LOVE

Subject The subject of Philemon is love.
Structure Philemon is in the form of an ancient letter with all the customary parts.

I. Salutation	1-3
II. Thanksgiving	4-5
III. Prayer	6-7
IV. The Body of the Letter	8-22
A. The Basis of Paul's Request	8-11
1. Not a Command	8
2. But Love	9-11
B. The Nature of Paul's Request	12-17
1. I wish I could Keep Him	13, 14
2. But I ask you to Receive Him	15, 17
C. The Payment for Paul's Request	18-22
1. The Payment	18, 19
2. The Profit	20-22
V. Personal Greetings	23-24
VI. Benediction	25

Author The author is Paul (vs. 1). He wrote it with his hand (vss. 1, 19). When Paul wrote this letter, he was in prison. He repeatedly refers to his chains (vss. 1, 9, 10, 13, 23). It is closely linked with Colossians. For example, Onesimus is specifically mentioned in Colossians (Col. 4:9), as are all the other people who sent greetings to Philemon (*cf.* vvs. 23, 24 with Col. 4:12, 10, 14). Thus, Paul wrote Philemon during his first Roman imprisonment in 60-62 AD. It was undoubtedly sent at the same time as Colossians, that is, in 61 AD.

Recipients The recipients were Philemon, Apphia, Archippus, and the church that met in Philemon's house. It is generally believed that Apphia was Philemon's wife and Archippus was the "pastor" of the church in his house (Col. 4:17). Some have suggested he was also Philemon's son, but there is no evidence for that. This is not a private letter. It was addressed to others, including the whole church. Onesimus was a slave of Philemon. He robbed his master and fled to Rome (vs. 18). He met Paul in the Imperial City and Paul led him to Christ (vs. 10). According to Roman law, Onesimus belonged to Philemon, so Paul sent him back.

Purpose The purpose was to request that Philemon receive Onesimus, a runaway slave, as a beloved brother and, if there was any debt, that it be put to his account. Philemon illustrates Christian love, forgiveness, and respect for the law.

Summary: The overall message is forgiving and restoring Onesimus, his runaway slave, is an illustration of Christian love.

The overall spiritual truth is as Christ loved us and paid for our sins so that we might be forgiven, we should love and forgive others even if we have to assume the cost.

Philemon 8-9 "Therefore, though I might be very bold in Christ to command you what is fitting, yet for love's sake I rather appeal *to you*—being such a one as Paul, the aged, and now also a prisoner of Jesus Christ."

Philemon 15-18 "For perhaps he departed for a while for this *purpose,* that you might receive him forever, no longer as a slave but more than a slave—a beloved brother, especially to me but how much more to you, both in the flesh and in the Lord. If then you count me as a partner, receive him as *you would* me. But if he has wronged you or owes anything, put that on my account."

It would be tempting to conclude that the subject of Philemon is the return of a runaway slave, but that would be like saying the subject of Hosea is the career of a prostitute. No doubt, the story's substance is slavery, but that is not the subject. Paul not only thanked God for Philemon's love, but it is a major emphasis of his thanksgiving (vss. 5-7). His appeal is based on love (vs. 9). His request was an act of love (see "receive him back" in vs. 12, "forever" in vs.. 15, and "as a beloved brother" in vs. 16). Notice also that in verse 20, he says, "Refresh my heart in the Lord" and, in verse 7, he said, "Your love has refreshed the heart of the saints." Luther said, "This epistle shows a right, noble, lovely example of Christian love." Paul requested that Philemon forgive and restore Onesimus, his runaway slave, as an illustration of Christian love. Christ loved us and paid for our sins that we might be forgiven. We should forgive others even if we have to assume the cost.

HEBREWS: THE SUPERIORITY OF CHRIST

Subject The subject of Hebrews is Jesus Christ, as the Son and King/Priest, is superior to Judaism.

Structure The literary structure is "distinctive" (Hiebert). It is generally classified as an epistle, but it lacks a salutation and begins more like an essay than an epistle. It ends like a letter. The contents suggest that it is a sermon cast into an epistolary form.

I. Prologue	1:1-4
II. Jesus is the Son/King	1:5-2:18
A. Jesus is the King; Angels are Servants	1:5-14
B. First Warning: Don't Neglect (Pay Attention)	2:1-4
C. Jesus is the Captain Who Suffered	2:5-18
D. Jesus is the Apostle; Moses was a Servant	3:1-6
E. Second Warning: Don't Harden Your Heart (Hold on)	3:7-4:13
III. Jesus is the Son/Priest	4:14-10:39
A. Jesus is Our High Priest	4:14-16
B. Jesus is Our Qualified High Priest	5:1-10
C. Third Warning: Don't Fall Away (Go to Maturity)	5:11-6:20
D. Jesus is Superior to Aaron	7:1-28
E. Jesus has Superior Covenant	8:1-9:10
F. Jesus' is a Superior Sacrifice	9:11-10:18
G. Fourth Warning: Don't Willfully Sin (Draw Near)	10:19-39
VI. Therefore, Live a Life of Faith	11:1-13:17
A. A Life of Faith Gains a Better Way	11:1-40
B. Endure like a Son	12:1-17
C. Fifth Warning: Don't Refuse to Hear (Serve Him)	12:18-29
D. Serve Acceptably	13:1-17
VII. Personal Greetings and Benediction	13:18-25

Author The author did not identify himself, but the original readers knew who he was (13:18-24). The two leading candidates are Paul and Barnabas. Paul signed all his letters (2 Thess. 3:17), but Hebrews is anonymous. All the arguments in favor of Paul fit Barnabas. 1) He was a Levite. 2) He was familiar with the teachings of Paul. 3) He knew Timothy. 4) This is a word of exhortation (13:22), the designation of Barnabas (Acts 4:36). 5) The earliest tradition (Tertullian) favors Barnabas. Origen said, "Who it was that really wrote the epistle, God only knows." When Hebrews was written, the sacrificial system was still operating (8:4; 13; 9:6-9; 10:1-3). Therefore, since the Temple was destroyed in 70 AD, Hebrews must have been written before 70 AD. Also, Hebrews mentions Timothy (13:23). If Paul is not the author, this suggests Paul was dead. Otherwise, Timothy would have been expected to join him. Hebrews was written between the death of Paul and the destruction of Jerusalem in 68 or 69 AD.

Recipients The recipients were Jewish Christians. There is no doubt that the recipients were believers ("we" in 2:3 and "holy brethren" in 3:1; also 3:12; 5:12-14; 6:1, 3, 5, 9; 10:22-23, and "we" in 26, 30, 35, 36; 12:4, 5) in a certain locality (3:7; 17-19; 22-24). They had been believers long enough to be teachers (5:12), had successfully endured persecution (10:32-34), and had financially assisted other Christians (6:10), but they were dull of hearing (5:11) and were in danger of drifting away (2:1; 3:12), that is, forsaking Christianity (10:25).

Purpose The purpose of Hebrews is to check their drift from Christ back to Judaism by showing that Christ is superior to Judaism and to challenge them to steadfastness and maturity. They are to be steadfast (3:14; 4:1, 14; 10:23-25, 35-36; 12:1-3) and mature (6:1; 4:16; 5:12-14) so they will be rewarded (10:35-36). As the divine king/priest, Jesus is superior to Judaism. [The word "better" occurs 13 times: 1:4; 6:9; 7:7, 19, 22; 8:6 (twice); 9:23; 10:34; 11:16, 35, 40, 12:24.]

Summary: The overall message is since Christ is the Son/King and Son/Priest, who is superior to Judaism, Jewish believers should not go back to Judaism but should, by faith, endure so that they will be rewarded.

The overall spiritual truth is that believers who, by faith, endure will grow to maturity and be rewarded.

Hebrews 3:12-13 "Beware, brethren, lest there be in any of you an evil heart of unbelief in departing from the living God; but exhort one another daily, while it is called 'TODAY,' lest any of you be hardened through the deceitfulness of sin."

Hebrews 4:12 "For the word of God is living and powerful, and sharper than any two-edged sword, piercing even to the division of soul and spirit, and of joints and marrow, and is a discerner of the thoughts and intents of the heart."

Hebrews 4:16 "Let us therefore come boldly to the throne of grace, that we may obtain mercy and find grace to help in time of need."

Hebrews 10:22-25 "let us draw near with a true heart in full assurance of faith, having our hearts sprinkled from an evil conscience and our bodies washed with pure water. Let us hold fast the confession of our hope without wavering, for He who promised is faithful. And let us consider one another in order to stir up love and good works, not forsaking the assembling of ourselves together, as is the manner of some, but exhorting one another, and so much the more as you see the Day approaching."

Hebrews 11:1 "Now faith is the substance of things hoped for, the evidence of things not seen."

Hebrews 12:1-2 "Therefore we also, since we are surrounded by so great a cloud of witnesses, let us lay aside every weight, and the sin which so easily ensnares us, and let us run with endurance the race that is set before us, looking unto Jesus, the author and finisher of our faith, who for the joy that was set before Him endured the cross, despising the shame, and has sat down at the right hand of the throne of God."

Hebrews 13:5 "Let your conduct be without covetousness; be content with such things as you have. For He Himself has said, "I WILL NEVER LEAVE YOU NOR FORSAKE YOU.""

Hebrews 13:15-16 "Therefore by Him let us continually offer the sacrifice of praise to God, that is, the fruit of our lips, giving thanks to His name.Hebrews. But do not forget to do good and to share, for with such sacrifices God is well pleased."

JAMES: HANDLING TRIALS

Subject The subject of James is trials.

Structure James is not a letter. Mant suggests the literary structure had a "sermonic origin." Whatever the literary form, the structure is summarized in James 1:19.

I.	Salutation	1:1
II.	Prologue	1:2-18
III.	Theme	1:19-20
IV.	Be Swift to Hear	1:21-2:26
	A. Hearing is Doing the Word	1:21-25
	B. Hearing is Practicing Mercy	1:26-2:13
	C. Hearing is Producing Works	2:14-26
V.	Be Slow to Speak	3:1-18
	A. Teaching and the tongue	3:1-12
	B. Wisdom and the tongue	3:13-18
VI.	Be Slow to Anger	4:1-5:12
	A. Conflicts	4:1-10
	B. Judging	4:11-12
	C. Planning	4:13-17
	D. Being treated unjustly	5:1-12
VII	Epilogue	5:13-20

Author James is the author (1:1). This half-brother of Jesus calls himself "a bondservant of God and the Lord Jesus Christ" (1:1). The "twelve tribes, which are scattered abroad" (1:1) is probably a reference to the Jewish Christians who were scattered abroad because of the persecution in Acts 8:4 (Acts 9:2; 11:19). If so, the date of James is about 45 AD.

Recipients The recipients were Jewish (1:1) Christians (2:1) who met in a synagogue ("assembly" in 2:2 is the Greek word "synagogue"). Strangers sometimes attended their meetings (2:2-4). Some were rich (1:10) and some were even traveling traders (4:13ff). The majority, however, were probably poor (1:9; 2:6; 5:1-6). They were having various kinds of trials. The rich were oppressing them by hauling them before the courts (2:6, 7) and wrongfully withholding their wages (5:4). These believers were also having trouble among themselves. They had disagreements, ambitions, and strife (3:13-18; 4:1, 2; 4:11). Some were weak from sickness (5:13).

Purpose The purpose was to exhort Christians to respond properly to trials and warn about the trials' dangers.

Summary: The overall message is the way to respond to trials is to trust God and learn from them by being swift to hear, that is, heed the Word, be slow to speak, and slow to anger.

The overall spiritual truth is in the midst of a trial, trust God, be swift to obey, slow to speak, and slow to get angry to obtain maximum maturity.

James 1:2-5 "My brethren, count it all joy when you fall into various trials, knowing that the testing of your faith produces patience. But let patience have *its* perfect work, that you may be perfect and complete, lacking nothing. If any of you lacks wisdom, let him ask of God, who gives to all liberally and without reproach, and it will be given to him."

James 1:19-20 "So then, my beloved brethren, let every man be swift to hear, slow to speak, slow to wrath; for the wrath of man does not produce the righteousness of God."

James 1:27 "Pure and undefiled religion before God and the Father is this: to visit orphans and widows in their trouble, *and* to keep oneself unspotted from the world."

James 2:8 "If you really fulfill *the* royal law according to the Scripture, 'You shall love your neighbor as yourself,' you do well."

James 2:10 "For whoever shall keep the whole law, and yet stumble in one *point*, he is guilty of all."

James 2:21 "Was not Abraham our father justified by works when he offered Isaac his son on the altar? Do you see that faith was working together with his works, and by works faith was made perfect?"

James 3:15-17 "This wisdom does not descend from above but *is* earthly, sensual, demonic. For where envy and self-seeking *exist*, confusion and every evil thing *are* there. But the wisdom that is from above is first pure, then peaceable, gentle, willing to yield, full of mercy and good fruits, without partiality and without hypocrisy."

James 4:1-3 "Where do wars and fights *come* from among you? Do *they* not *come* from your *desires for* pleasure that war in your members? You lust and do not have. You murder and covet and cannot obtain. You fight and war. Yet you do not have because you do not ask. You ask and do not receive, because you ask amiss, that you may spend *it* on your pleasures."

James 4:6 "But He gives more grace. Therefore He says: 'God resists the proud, but gives grace to the humble.'"

James 4:17 "Therefore, to him who knows to do good and does not do *it*, to him it is si

James 5:9 "Do not grumble against one another, brethren, lest you be condemned. Behold, the Judge is standing at the door!"

James 5:19-20 "Brethren, if anyone among you wanders from the truth, and someone turns him back, let him know that he who turns a sinner from the error of his way will save a soul from death and cover a multitude of sins."

1 PETER: THE SALVATION OF THE SOUL

Subject The subject of 1 Peter is the "salvation of the soul," meaning "life" (1:9).
Structure First Peter is a letter. Only the "prayer" is missing.

I. Salutation	1:1-2
II. Thanksgiving	1:3-12
III. The Body of the Letter	1:13-5:9
A. Salvation of the Soul in Relation to God	1:13-21
1. Hope	1:13
2. Holiness	1:14-16
3. Heavenly Fear	1:17-21
B. Salvation of the Soul in Relation to the Church (believers)	1:22-2:10
1. Love the Brethren	1:22-25
2. Desire the Word	2:1-10
C. Salvation of the Soul in Relation to the World	2:11-3:7
1. Through Abstinence from Lust	2:11-12
2. Through Subjection	2:13-3:7
D. Salvation of the Soul in Relation to Life	3:8-4:6
1. Through Blessing	3:8-12
2. Through Suffering	3:13-4:6
E. Salvation of the Soul in Relation to the End	4:7-5:9
1. Through Service	4:7-11
2. Through Suffering	4:12-19
3. Through Shepherding	5:1-4
4. Through Submission	5:5-9
IV. Personal Greetings and Benediction	5:10-14

Author The author of 1 Peter was Peter (1:1). The book mentions suffering, but there is no evidence it was the persecution of Nero that resulted in martyrdom. Therefore, the epistle was written on the eve of Nero's persecution. The date is either late 63 or early 64 AD.

Recipients The recipients were "the pilgrims of the dispersion" (1:1). That, plus the injunction to keep their behavior "excellent among the Gentiles" (2:12), gives the impression that the readers were Jewish Christians. Yet the content indicates they were Gentiles (2:9, 10 and 1:14, 18; 4:3-4). Both conclusions are right. The Gentiles were probably in the majority. These Jewish and Gentile believers lived in Asia Minor in regions not mentioned in Acts (Pontus, Cappadocia, and Bithynia; 1:1). They were experiencing opposition (1:6; 3:13-17; 4:12-19; 5:9-10), were being slandered and attacked because of their faith (4:14-15), and were being charged with disloyalty to the state (2:13-17). Peter calls these "fiery trials" (4:12).

Purpose The purpose is to exhort (5:12). There are 34 imperatives in the book. Peter exhorts believers to holiness, love, growth, submission, service, etc., all of which can be summarized as salvation (1:9) or the grace of God (5:12). He also wrote to testify (5:12). His exhortation to stand fast in the faith constitutes his testimony to the fact that this is the true grace of God (5:12).

They were facing and would face in future persecution (3:14), suffering, and fiery trials (4:12). Such pressure would (no doubt) tempt them to doubt, to be fainthearted, and to fail. Peter assures them that they are right despite the opposition they are experiencing.

Summary: The overall message is believers save their lives from fleshly lust by submitting to the will of God, even in the face of suffering.

The overall spiritual truth is believers save themselves from spiritual damage by living a holy, loving, submissive, serving life even while suffering.

1 Peter 1:6-7 "In this you greatly rejoice, though now for a little while, if need be, you have been grieved by various trials, that the genuineness of your faith, being much more precious than gold that perishes, though it is tested by fire, may be found to praise, honor, and glory at the revelation of Jesus Christ."

1 Peter 1:13-16 "Therefore gird up the loins of your mind, be sober, and rest your hope fully upon the grace that is to be brought to you at the revelation of Jesus Christ; as obedient children, not conforming yourselves to the former lusts, as in your ignorance; but as He who called you is holy, you also be holy in all your conduct, because it is written, 'Be holy, for I am holy.'"

1 Peter 2:1-3 "Therefore, laying aside all malice, all deceit, hypocrisy, envy, and all evil speaking, as newborn babes, desire the pure milk of the word, that you may grow thereby, if indeed you have tasted that the Lord is gracious."

1 Peter 3:18 "For Christ also suffered once for sins, the just for the unjust, that He might bring us to God, being put to death in the flesh but made alive by the Spirit."

1 Peter 4:12-13 "Beloved, do not think it strange concerning the fiery trial which is to try you, as though some strange thing happened to you; but rejoice to the extent that you partake of Christ's sufferings, that when His glory is revealed, you may also be glad with exceeding joy."

1 Peter 4:15 "But let none of you suffer as a murderer, a thief, an evildoer, or as a busybody in other people's matters."

1 Peter 5:6-8 "Therefore humble yourselves under the mighty hand of God, that He may exalt you in due time, casting all your care upon Him, for He cares for you. Be sober, be vigilant; because your adversary the devil walks about like a roaring lion, seeking whom he may devour."

2 PETER: THE SECOND COMING OF CHRIST

Structure

Subject The subject of 2 Peter is the Second Coming of Christ.

Structure Second Peter is basically in the form of an ancient letter. It has a salutation, a body, and a benediction, but no prayer of thanksgiving

I. Salutation	1:1, 2
II. Prologue: Promises make Godliness Possible and Profitable	1:3-11
III. The Body of the Letter	1:12-3:13
A. The Promises of Prophecies are Sure	1:12-21
B. The Perversions of False Teachers will be Judged	2:1-22
1. Judgment	2:1-9
2. Their Nature	2:10-17
3. Their Allurements	2:18-22
C. The Pronouncements of Scoffers are Wrong	3:1-13
1. Scoffers will Deny the Second Coming	3:1-7
2. The Lord is not slack concerning His Promises	3:8-10
3. Therefore, We should live Godly Lives	3:11-13
IV. Conclusion	3:14-18

Author The author 2 Peter was Peter (1:1; 3:1; see also 1:16-18). Second Peter 1:14 seems to indicate the letter was written just prior to his death, which was probably in 64 AD. So, 2 Peter was probably written in 64 AD.

Recipients Second Peter 3:1 seems to suggest that Peter had in mind the same readers of Asia Minor as he did in 1 Peter, although the more general salutation of 2 Peter 1:1 would allow for a wider audience. The occasion of this epistle was false teachers who "were coming" in the future (2:1; 3:3). Peter begins by talking about precious promises (1:4). Chapter 3 seems to describe these promises as Christ's coming (3:4, 9, 13). Furthermore, he talks about the coming of the Lord in chapter 1 (1:16) and at the end of chapter 3 (3:4, 10, 12). False teachers and scoffers will deny the Second Coming of Christ (3:4), live a lustful lifestyle (3:3, 2:10, 14), and lead others, even believers, astray (2:14).

Purpose The purpose was to warn against false teachers and scoffers, to remind them of what they knew, and to exhort them to heed it so they would grow (3:17-18).

Summary: The overall message is the Lord is coming back, so avoid the coming false teachers and scoffers and grow in the grace and knowledge of Jesus Christ.

The overall spiritual truth is in light of the return of the Lord, believers should avoid false teachers and scoffers and live godly lives.

2 Peter 1:5-11 "But also for this very reason, giving all diligence, add to your faith virtue, to virtue knowledge, to knowledge self-control, to self-control perseverance, to perseverance godliness, to godliness brotherly kindness, and to brotherly kindness love. For if these things are yours and abound, *you will be* neither barren nor unfruitful in the knowledge of our Lord Jesus Christ. For he who lacks these things is shortsighted, even to blindness, and has forgotten that he was cleansed from his old sins. Therefore, brethren, be even more diligent to make your call and election sure, for if you do these things you will never stumble; for so an entrance will be supplied to you abundantly into the everlasting kingdom of our Lord and Savior Jesus Christ."

2 Peter 1:16 "For we did not follow cunningly devised fables when we made known to you the power and coming of our Lord Jesus Christ, but were eyewitnesses of His majesty."

2 Peter 2:1 "But there were also false prophets among the people, even as there will be false teachers among you, who will secretly bring in destructive heresies, even denying the Lord who bought them, *and* bring on themselves swift destruction."

2 Peter 3:9 "The Lord is not slack concerning *His* promise, as some count slackness, but is longsuffering toward us, not willing that any should perish but that all should come to repentance."

2 Peter 3:17-18 "You therefore, beloved, since you know *this* beforehand, beware lest you also fall from your own steadfastness, being led away with the error of the wicked; but grow in the grace and knowledge of our Lord and Savior Jesus Christ. To Him *be* the glory both now and forever. Amen."

1 JOHN: FELLOWSHIP WITH THE TRUE GOD

Subject The subject of 1 John is fellowship (1:3).

Structure First John does not have the elements of an ancient letter, such as a salutation, thanksgiving, prayer, etc. It is more like an essay.

I.	Prologue	1:1-4
II.	Fellowship with God who is Light	1:5-2:28
	A. The Provision for Fellowship	1:5-2:2
	B. The Proof for Fellowship	2:3-11
	C. The Position of the Readers	2:12-14
	D. The Preventatives to Fellowship	2:15-28
	1. Love for the World	2:15-17
	2. Listening to False Prophets	2:18-28
III.	Fellowship with God who is Righteous	2:29-4:6
	A. The Manifestation of God's Children	2:29-4:6
	B. The Manifestation of Righteousness	3:10b-24
	1. What Love is not	3:10b-15
	2. What Love is	3:16-18
	3. What Love does	3:19-24
	C. The Manifestation of the Spirit of Truth	4:1-6
IV.	Fellowship with God who is Love	4:7-5:13
	A. Reasons for Love	4:7-21
	B. Power for Love	5:1-13
	C. Practice of Love	5:14-17
V.	Epilogue	5:18-21

Author The author is anonymous. He was an eyewitness to the earthly life of Christ (1:1-2), and he calls himself an apostle (in 1:1-3; 4:14, "we" equals apostles, "you" are the readers, and "they" are the false teachers). First John was probably written between 67 and 90 AD, maybe about 80 AD.

Recipients John wrote to believers (2:12-14, 21; 5:13). There was no doubt in his mind that they were Christians (2:1, 12, 28; 3:7, 18; 4:4; 5:21; also 2:12, 18 and see "brethren" in 2:7; 3:13 and "beloved" in 3:2, 21; 4:1, 7, 11). They had been believers for a long time (there was nothing new to offer them; 2:7, 18, 20, 21, 24, 27; 3:11). He may even be addressing leaders. He tells them that they possess an anointing and do not need teachers (2:20, 27), which implies they were spiritually mature since the immature need human teachers (Heb. 5:12). Even so, the book was to be read by all. They were confronted with many false teachers ("antichrists;" 2:18-26; 4:1) who originated in Judea (2:19) and denied that Jesus was the Christ (2:22). Apparently, this was a denial of the incarnation. They probably claimed to have the Father while denying the truth of the Son (2:22, 23).

Purpose The purpose was to promote fellowship (1:3), to prevent sin (2:1), to proclaim forgiveness (2:12), to protect the saints (2:26), and to provide assurance (5:13). The first of these is the purpose of the whole book. The others refer to their immediate context.

Summary: The overall message is believers should maintain their fellowship with the Lord and manifest their faith through correct doctrine, righteous living, and wholehearted love for the brethren.

The overall spiritual truth is that believers are to abide in what they heard from the beginning to maintain their fellowship with God and love for the brethren.

1 John 1:3-4 "That which we have seen and heard we declare to you, that you also may have fellowship with us; and truly our fellowship *is* with the Father and with His Son Jesus Christ. And these things we write to you that your joy may be full."

1 John 1:5 "This is the message which we have heard from Him and declare to you, that God is light and in Him is no darkness at all."

1 John 1:9 "If we confess our sins, He is faithful and just to forgive us *our* sins and to cleanse us from all unrighteousness."

1 John 2:1-2 "My little children, these things I write to you, so that you may not sin. And if anyone sins, we have an Advocate with the Father, Jesus Christ the righteous. And He Himself is the propitiation for our sins, and not for ours only but also for the whole world."

1 John 2:15-16 "Do not love the world or the things in the world. If anyone loves the world, the love of the Father is not in him. For all that *is* in the world—the lust of the flesh, the lust of the eyes, and the pride of life—is not of the Father but is of the world."

1 John 2:28 "And now, little children, abide in Him, that when He appears, we may have confidence and not be ashamed before Him at His coming.

1 John 3:9-11 "Whoever has been born of God does not sin, for His seed remains in him; and he cannot sin, because he has been born of God. In this the children of God and the children of the devil are manifest: Whoever does not practice righteousness is not of God, nor *is* he who does not love his brother. For this is the message that you heard from the beginning, that we should love one another."

1 John 3:20 "For if our heart condemns us, God is greater than our heart, and knows all things."

1 John 3:23-24 "And this is His commandment: that we should believe on the name of His Son Jesus Christ and love one another, as He gave us commandment. Now he who keeps His commandments abides in Him, and He in him. And by this we know that He abides in us, by the Spirit whom He has given us."

1 John 4:17 "Love has been perfected among us in this: that we may have boldness in the day of judgment; because as He is, so are we in this world."

1 John 5:13 "These things I have written to you who believe in the name of the Son of God, that you may know that you have eternal life, and that you may *continue to* believe in the name of the Son of God."

2 JOHN: THE TRUTH OF GOD

Subject The subject 2 John is truth (see vs. 1 where it appears twice and vss. 2, 3, and 4). Other verses talk about truth but do not use the word (for example, vss. 5, 6, 7, 9).

Structure Second John follows the format of an ancient letter, except it does not have the thanksgiving, prayer, or benediction. The body is divided into two parts: exhortation and warning.

I.	Salutation	1-3
II.	The Body of the Letter	4-11
	A. The Practice of Truth	4-6
	1. The Walk in Truth	4
	2. The Walk in Love	5-6
	B. The Protection of Truth	7-11
	1. The Danger	7
	2. The Duty	8-11
III.	Personal Greetings	12-13

Author The author was the elder (vs. 1). The similarities between 2 John and 1 John, as well as tradition, lead to the conclusion that the author was the apostle John. Most reason that 1 and 2 John deal with the same problem and use similar (in some cases identical) material. Therefore, they were written at about the same time. So, 2 John was probably written between 67 and 90 AD, maybe about 80 AD.

Recipients The recipients were an elect lady and her children. There are two basic interpretations of this phrase: 1) that it refers to an individual Christian lady; 2) that it is used figuratively of a church. The content and the use of the plural in verses 6-12 are most appropriate to a community. Also, consider that if the lady's name is Electa, she had a sister by the same name (vs.13). Furthermore, if an actual Christian woman were addressed, the greeting would have come from her sister and not from her sister's children (vs. 13). The recipients were faced with false teachers (vs. 7). John instructed the church not to be deceived by them (vs. 8), to receive them (vs. 10a), nor to greet them (vs. 10b). If they greeted them and received them, they would deceive them. If they deceived them, they would cease obeying God and loving others (vs. 6).

Purpose The purpose was to exhort a local church to practice the truth (vs. 5) and to warn a local church about the perverters of truth. They were in danger of not receiving a full reward (vs. 8). If they did not abide in the doctrine of Christ, they would lose out at the Judgment Seat of Christ. In short, John wrote this letter for the practice and purity of the truth.

Summary: The overall message is continue practicing the truth and do not receive deceivers. The overall spiritual truth is believers should walk in truth and not support deceivers of the truth.

2 John 1:8 "Look to yourselves, that we do not lose those things we worked for, but *that* we may receive a full reward."

Verse 10 has been greatly misunderstood. It says, If anyone comes to you and does not bring this doctrine, do not receive him into your house nor greet him." This verse has been interpreted to mean you should never let cultists into your house, but that is not the point. "House" is the church, which in that day met in homes. "Coming" is not the casual visit of a stranger but the coming of a teacher claiming authority. "Receive" means to let him speak and to support him, including giving him hospitality. Don't even greet him (literally, "to rejoice or be glad"),I which means, "Don't say, 'I'm glad to see you. I wish you well.'" It has been suggested that all this means that they should make it plain from their aloofness that in no way they condoned the activities of these men.

3 JOHN: THE PRACTICE OF LOVE

Subject The subject of 3 John is love (vs. 5). In John's thought, truth is the foundation of love (vs. 2:3-11, esp. 2:4, 7ff; 3:19). Hospitality is one expression of love. In 3 John, Gaius loves others (vs. 6) and Diotrephes loves himself (vs. 9).

Structure Third John follows the formula of an ancient letter. It contains a salutation, prayer, body, and ends with personal greetings and benediction. Only the customary thanksgiving is omitted (though John does express joy for Gaius).

I.	Salutation	1
II.	Prayer	2-4
III.	The Body of the Letter	5-12
	A. Confirmation of Gaius	5-8
	1. His Example of Hospitality	5-6
	2. The Explanation for Hospitality	7-8
	B. Condemnation of Diotrephes	9-11
	1. His Actions	9-10
	2. Your Reactions	11
	C. Commendation of Demetrius	12
IV.	Personal Greeting and Benediction	13-14

Author The author identifies himself as "the elder," referring to the apostle John (see 2 Jn.). Third John was probably written between 67 and 90 AD, maybe about 80 AD (see 2 Jn.).

Recipient The recipient was Gaius. John sent out teachers. A team of teachers arrived with a letter of commendation from John, but a fellow named Diotrephes refused them and John's letter (vs. 9). They returned to John and reported the hostility of Diotrephes and the hospitality of Gaius. John had led Gaius to Christ (vs. 4), and they were close friends (vs. 1). So John wrote to this wealthy layman to encourage him to continue receiving missionaries despite Diotrephes' opposition. He also announced his intention to visit to deal with the situation personally.

Purpose The purpose was to encourage Gaius to continue doing what he was doing (vs. 5-6) and tell him not to imitate Diotrephes (vs. 11); John would deal with him when he arrived (vs. 10). John also wrote to endorse Demetrius. Demetrius may have just been the bearer of the letter, the postman, but, on the other hand, he may have been one of the traveling teachers. Either way, he would need hospitality. So John writes to endorse him in the highest possible terms.

Summary: The overall message is to continue the practice of love in the form of hospitality. The overall spiritual truth is hospitality is an important form of love.

3 John 2 "Beloved, I pray that you may prosper in all things and be in health, just as your soul prospers."

3 John 4 "I have no greater joy than to hear that my children walk in truth."

3 John 9 "I wrote to the church, but Diotrephes, who loves to have the preeminence among them, does not receive us."

JUDE: FALSE TEACHERS

Subject The subject of Jude is false teachers.

Structure The literary structure is basically that of an ancient letter, but it does not have the customary thanksgiving, prayer, and personal greetings. The body of the book is divided into two parts, each beginning with a reference (in triplet) to the Old Testament (vss. 5-7 and 11). Each Old Testament section is applied to the infiltrators ("these," vss. 8, 10 and 12, 16, 19).

I. Salutation	1-2
II. Prologue	3-4
III. The Body of the Letter	5-23
A. Sinners will be Judged	5-10
1. Sinners in the Old Testament were Judged	5-7
2. Likewise, these Sinners will be Judged	8-10
B. False Teachers will be Judged	11-23
1. They are Unbelievers	11
2. Their Characteristics	12-15
3. Their Conversation	16-18
4. Their Constitution	19-23
IV. Doxology	24-25

Author The author is Jude, the servant of Jesus Christ and a brother of James (vs. 1). That means he is the half-brother of the Lord (Mt. 13:55 and Mk. 6:2). Two of the half-brothers of the Lord wrote Scripture: James and Jude. Both call themselves His slave. Peter predicted the coming of false teachers (2 Pet. 2:1; 2; 3:3) and Jude recorded the fulfillment of Peter's prophecy (vss. 4, 11, 12, 17, 18). Jude quotes 2 Peter 3:3 (vs. 8). Therefore, Jude could not have been written before 64 AD, the year Peter wrote his second epistle. It is likely that some years passed between the prediction in 2 Peter and the fulfillment in Jude. Jude was probably written about 75 AD.

Recipients The recipients were believers in general (vs. 1). Nevertheless, Jude had a specific group in mind. They were troubled by ungodly men (vs. 4), who were infiltrators into their love feasts (vs. 12). These men were false teachers (vs. 8). These false teachers were libertines (vs. 4). Jude calls them dreamers (vs. 8), which suggests the possibility that they claimed prophetic visions. He does not doubt that they were ungodly men (vs. 4, 5-10, 15, 18, etc.) headed for judgment (vs. 13, 14-15).

Purpose The purposes were to remind believers that God will judge the ungodly and to encourage believers to contend for the faith (vs. 3). The Greek word translated "contend" means "to contend for a prize, fight, struggle, strive."

Summary: The overall message is God will judge the ungodly, including false teachers, and believers should contend for the faith.

The overall spiritual truth is God will judge the ungodly and believers should contend for the faith.

Jude 1:3 "Beloved, while I was very diligent to write to you concerning our common salvation, I found it necessary to write to you exhorting you to contend earnestly for the faith which was once for all delivered to the saints."

Jude 1:20-23 "But you, beloved, building yourselves up on your most holy faith, praying in the Holy Spirit, keep yourselves in the love of God, looking for the mercy of our Lord Jesus Christ unto eternal life. And on some have compassion, making a distinction; but others save with fear, pulling *them* out of the fire, hating even the garment defiled by the flesh.

Jude 1:24-25 "Now to Him who is able to keep you from stumbling, And to present *you* faultless Before the presence of His glory with exceeding joy, to God our Savior, Who alone is wise, Be glory and majesty, Dominion and power, Both now and forever. Amen."

How do believers contend for the faith? Most of Jude deals with ungodly infiltrators into the love feasts of the believers, but toward the end, he begins to speak directly to the readers. Since he begins by saying that he is writing to exhort them to contend for the faith, his exhortations must be about how to contend for the faith.

The exhortations include: 1) Remember: mockers will come living ungodly lives (vss. 17-18). 2) Remain: keep yourself in the love of God (vss. 20-21). Jude 20-21 consists of one command ("keep yourself in the love of God") and three participles (building, praying, looking). The way to keep yourself in the love of God is by "building, praying, looking" (Jn. 15:10). 3) Rescue others (keep yourself in the love of God, vss. 22-23). While some take these verses to be referring to unsaved people, they are written to believers. (The majority of Greek manuscripts contain "them" in vs. 24.) Believers are to rescue other believers from ungodly living (vss. 24-25; Gal. 6:1; Jas. 5:19-20).

REVELATION: JUDGMENT BY JESUS CHRIST

Subject The subject of Revelation is judgment by Jesus Christ.

Structure Revelation is a blend of epistolary and apocalyptic literature. Apocalyptic literature uses symbols that are often arbitrary. The literary structure is given in Revelation 1:9 and 4:1: things seen (1:9-20), things which are (2-3), and things which will take place after this (4-22).

I. Prologue	1:1-8
II. Christ Revealed as Judge	1:9-20
III. Christ Revealed as Judge of the Church	2:1-3:22
A. To Ephesus	2:1-7
B. To Smyrna	2:8-11
C. To Pergamos	2:12-17
D. To Thyatira	2:18-29
E. To Sardis	3:1-6
F. To Philadelphia	3:7-13
G. To Laodicea	3:14-22
IV. Christ Revealed as Judge of the World	4:1-22:5
A. Introduction: The Judge	4:1-5:14
B. The Seven Seal Judgments	6:1-8:1
C. The Seven Trumpet Judgments	8:2-11:19
D. The Explanatory Prophecies	12:1-14:20
E. The Seven Bowl Judgments	15:1-16:21
F. The Judgment of Babylon	17, 18
G. The Second Coming	19:1-21
H. The Millennium	20:1-10
V. The Great White Throne Judgment	20:11-15
VI. The New Heavens and the New Earth	21:1-22:5
VII. Epilogue	22:6-20
VIII. Benediction	22:21

Author The author is John (1:1, 1:4, 1:9; 22:8), "a servant of Christ" (1:1), and "your brother and companion in tribulation" (1:9). Tradition says the author was John, the apostle. He was banished to Patmos (1:9) and wrote before his release (1:11; 22:7, 9, 10, 18, 19). Ancient writers say John was banished to Patmos in the 15th year of Domitian, who ruled 80-95 AD and Nerva released him (96 AD). Therefore, John wrote Revelation in 95 or 96 AD.

Recipients The recipients were the seven churches of Asia Minor (1:4, 10, 11; 22:16).

Purpose The purpose is to comfort persecuted Christians and challenge complacent Christians.

Summary: The overall message is since Jesus Christ is the Judge of the churches, as well as the world, persecuted Christians should be comforted and complacent Christians should be challenged to endure so they will be rewarded.

The overall spiritual truth is that persecuted Christians should be comforted and complacent Christians should be challenged to endure so they will be rewarded.

Revelation 1:3 "Blessed *is* he who reads and those who hear the words of this prophecy, and keep those things which are written in it; for the time *is* near."

Revelation 1:19 "Write the things which you have seen, and the things which are, and the things which will take place after this."

Revelation 2:4-5 "Nevertheless I have *this* against you, that you have left your first love. Remember, therefore from where you have fallen; repent and do the first works, or else I will come to you quickly and remove your lampstand from its place—unless you repent."

Revelation 2:26-28 "And he who overcomes, and keeps My works until the end, to him I will give power over the nations.'He shall rule them with a rod of iron; they shall be dashed to pieces like the potter's vessels'—as I also have received from My Father; and I will give him the morning star."

Revelation 3:20 "Behold, I stand at the door and knock. If anyone hears My voice and opens the door, I will come in to him and dine with him, and he with Me."

Revelation 6:9-10 "When He opened the fifth seal, I saw under the altar the souls of those who had been slain for the word of God and for the testimony which they held. And they cried with a loud voice, saying, 'How long, O Lord, holy and true, until You judge and avenge our blood on those who dwell on the earth?'"

Revelation 16:5-7 "And I heard the angel of the waters saying: 'You are righteous, O Lord, The One who is and who was and who is to be, Because You have judged these things. For they have shed the blood of saints and prophets, And You have given them blood to drink. For it is their just due.' And I heard another from the altar saying, "Even so, Lord God Almighty, true and righteous *are* Your judgments.

Revelation 19:11 "Now I saw heaven opened, and behold, a white horse. And He who sat on him *was* called Faithful and True, and in righteousness He judges and makes war."

Revelation 20:4 "And I saw thrones, and they sat on them, and judgment was committed to them. Then *I saw* the souls of those who had been beheaded for their witness to Jesus and for the word of God, who had not worshiped the beast or his image, and had not received *his* mark on their foreheads or on their hands. And they lived and reigned with Christ for a thousand years."

Revelation 21:1-2 "Now I saw a new heaven and a new earth, for the first heaven and the first earth had passed away. Also, there was no more sea. Then I, John, saw the holy city, New Jerusalem, coming down out of heaven from God, prepared as a bride adorned for her husband.

Revelation 21:8 "But the cowardly, unbelieving, abominable, murderers, sexually immoral, sorcerers, idolaters, and all liars shall have their part in the lake which burns with fire and brimstone, which is the second death."

Revelation 22:12 "And behold, I am coming quickly, and My reward *is* with Me, to give to everyone according to his work."

Revelation 22:20 "He who testifies to these things says, 'Surely I am coming quickly.' Amen. Even so, come, Lord Jesus!"

The Old Testament

Genesis	Moses	1447 BC	Exodus generation	Election
Exodus	Moses	1446 BC	Exodus generation	Redemption
Leviticus	Moses	1446 BC	Exodus generation	Holiness
Numbers	Moses	1407 BC	Second generation	Faithfulness
Deuteronomy	Moses	1407 BC	Second generation	Obedience
Joshua	Joshua	1400 BC	Second generation	Possessions
Judges	Samuel	1040 BC	Jews at the time	Departure
Ruth	Samuel	1015 BC	Jews at the time	Kinsman
1 Samuel	Samuel, etc.	925 BC	Jews at the time	Establishment
2 Samuel	Nathan & Gad.	925 BC	Jews at the time	Expansion
1 Kings	Jeremiah/sources	600/570 BC	Jews in Babylon	Division
2 Kings	Jeremiah/sources	600/570 BC	Jews in Babylon	Destruction
1 Chronicle	Ezra/sources	450 BC	Jews from Babylon	Preparation
2 Chronicles	Ezra/sources	450 BC	Jews from Babylon	Building
Ezra	Ezra/sources	450 BC	Jews from Babylon	Restoration
Nehemiah	Nehemiah	425 BC	Jews from Babylon	Continual
Esther	Mordechai	464/435 BC	Jews in Persia	Providence
Job	Job	2000/1800 BC	People at the time	Suffering
Psalms	Seven authors	1407/580 BC	Jews at the time	Praise
Proverbs	Four authors	950/710 BC	His son, etc., 1:8	Wisdom
Ecclesiastes	Solomon	935 BC	His son, etc., 12:12	Futility
Song of Solomon	Solomon	970 BC	Jews at the time	Romantic love
Isaiah	Isaiah	680 BC	Southern kingdom	Salvation
Jeremiah	Jeremiah	580 BC	Jews in Babylon	Judgment
Lamentations	Jeremiah	586 BC	Jews in Jerusalem	Lamentations
Ezekiel	Ezekiel	565 BC	Jews in Babylon	Glory of God
Daniel	Daniel	530 BC	Jews in Babylon	Sovereignty
Hosea	Hosea	725 BC	Northern Kingdom	Love of God
Joel	Joel	830 BC	Southern kingdom	Day of the Lord
Amos	Amos	760 BC	Northern Kingdom	Judgment
Obadiah	Obadiah	850 BC	Southern kingdom	Edom
Jonah	Jonah	760 BC	Not stated/Israel	Nineveh/grace
Micah	Micah	735 BC	Both kingdoms	Summons
Nahum	Nahum	655 BC	Southern kingdom	Nineveh
Habakkuk	Habakkuk	607 BC	Southern kingdom	Righteousness
Zephaniah	Zephaniah	630/625 BC	Southern kingdom	Day of the Lord
Haggai	Haggai	520 BC	Jews in Jerusalem	Rebuilding
Zechariah	Zechariah	520/480 BC	Jews in Jerusalem	Restore Jer.
Malachi	Malachi	430 BC	People/priests/etc.	Charges

Chronologically, the first prophet to write was Obadiah (850 BC) and the second was Joel (830 BC). Hosea (725 BC) and Amos (760 BC) wrote to the Northern Kingdom and Jonah (760 BC) and Micah (735 BC) wrote to both kingdoms. Isaiah (680 BC), Nahum (655 BC), Habakkuk (607 BC), and Zephaniah (630/625 BC) ministered in the Southern Kingdom. Jeremiah (580 BC) and Lamentations (586 BC), Haggai (520 BC), Zechariah (520 BC), and Malachi (430 BC) prophesied to the Jews in Jerusalem who had returned from Babylon.

The New Testament

Book	Author	Date	Audience	Theme
Matthew	Matthew	45-50 A.D.	Jewish believers	King
Mark	John Mark	61-67 A.D.	Roman believers	Servant
Luke	Luke	59 A.D.	Theophilus	Humanity
John	John	before 70 A.D.	Unbelievers, plus	Deity
Acts	Luke	61 A.D.	Theophilus	Spread/gospel
Romans	Paul	57 A.D.	Church in Rome	Righteousness
1 Corinthians	Paul	57 A.D.	Church in Corinth	Disorder
2 Corinthians	Paul	57 A.D.	Church in Corinth	True ministry
Galatians	Paul	49 A.D.	Churches in Galatia	Freedom
Ephesians	Paul	61 A.D.	Church in Ephesus	Calling
Philippians	Paul, Timothy	62 A.D.	Church in Philippi	Living worthy
Colossians	Paul	61 A.D.	Church in Colosse	Sufficiency
1 Thessalonians	Paul, Silas, Tim	51 A.D.	Church in Thess.	Sanctification
2 Thessalonians	Paul, Silas, Tim	51 A.D.	Church in Thess.	Correction
1 Timothy	Paul	62 A.D.	Timothy/church	Conduct
2 Timothy	Paul	67 A.D.	Timothy	Ministry/Word
Titus	Paul	62 A.D.	Titus	Order in churches
Philemon	Paul	61 A.D.	Philemon, etc.	An example
Hebrews	Barnabas	68/69 A.D.	Jewish Christians	Superiority
James	James	45 A.D.	Jewish Christians	Trials
1 Peter	Peter	63/64 A.D.	Pilgrims/dispersion	Salvation/soul
2 Peter	Peter	64 A.D.	Believers	Second Coming
1 John	John	67-90 80 A.D.	Believers/leaders	Fellowship
2 John	Elder/John	67-90 80 A.D.	Elect lady/children	Truth of God
3 John	John	67-90 80 A.D.	Garius	Practice of Love
Jude	Jude	75 A.D.	Believers	False Teaching
Revelation	John	95 A.D.	Seven churches	Judgment

www.ingramcontent.com/pod-product-compliance
Lightning Source LLC
Chambersburg PA
CBHW081453070526
44586CB00019B/2333